HEINRICH BULLINGER

CASCADE COMPANIONS

The Christian theological tradition provides an embarrassment of riches: from Scripture to modern scholarship, we are blessed with a vast and complex theological inheritance. And yet this feast of traditional riches is too frequently inaccessible to the general reader.

The Cascade Companions series addresses the challenge by publishing books that combine academic rigor with broad appeal and readability. They aim to introduce nonspecialist readers to that vital storehouse of authors, documents, themes, histories, arguments, and movements that comprise this heritage with brief yet compelling volumes.

SOME OTHER TITLES IN THIS SERIES:

Cascade Companion to Evil by Charles Taliaferro
Reading Paul by Michael Gorman
The Rule of Faith by Everett Ferguson
The Second-Century Apologists by Alvyn Pettersen
Origen by Ronald E. Heine
Athanasius of Alexandria by Lois Farag
Basil of Caesarea by Andrew Radde-Gallwitz
Reading Augustine by Jason Byassee
A Guide to St Symeon the New Theologian by Hannah Hunt
Thomas à Kempis by Greg Peters
Lutheran Theology by Paul R. Hinlicky
John Calvin by Donald K. McKim
Jacob Arminius by Rustin E. Brian
Richard Hooker by W. Bradford Littlejohn
John Wesley by Henry H. Knight III
A Companion to Mercersburg Theology by William B. Evans
Reading Kierkegaard I by Paul Martens
Reading Bonhoeffer by John W. Matthews
Rudolph Bultmann by David W. Congdon
Jacques Ellul by Jacob E. Van Vleet and Jacob M. Rollinson
Understanding Pannenberg by Anthony C. Thiselton
Queer Theology by Linn Marie Tonstad

HEINRICH BULLINGER

An Introduction to His Life and Theology

DONALD K. McKIM
and JIM WEST

CASCADE Books • Eugene, Oregon

HEINRICH BULLINGER
An Introduction to His Life and Theology

Copyright © 2022 Donald K. McKim and Jim West. All rights reserved. Except for brief quotations in critical publications or reviews, no part of this book may be reproduced in any manner without prior written permission from the publisher. Write: Permissions, Wipf and Stock Publishers, 199 W. 8th Ave., Suite 3, Eugene, OR 97401.

Cascade Books
An Imprint of Wipf and Stock Publishers
199 W. 8th Ave., Suite 3
Eugene, OR 97401

www.wipfandstock.com

PAPERBACK ISBN: 978-1-6667-3257-3
HARDCOVER ISBN: 978-1-6667-2643-5
EBOOK ISBN: 978-1-6667-2644-2

Cataloguing-in-Publication data:

Names: McKim, Donald K. [author]. | West, Jim [author] | Campi, Emidio [foreword writer]

Title: Heinrich Bullinger : an introduction to his life and thought / Donald K. McKim and Jim West.

Description: Eugene, OR: Cascade Books, 2022 | Series: Cascade Companions Series | Includes bibliographical references.

Identifiers: ISBN 978-1-6667-3257-3 (paperback) | ISBN 978-1-6667-2643-5 (hardcover) | ISBN 978-1-6667-2644-2 (ebook)

Subjects: LCSH: Bullinger, Heinrich, 1504–1575 | Reformation—Switzerland | Theologians—Switzerland—History—16th century | Reformation| Switzerland—Church history—16th century

Classification: BR350.B9 M35 2022 (paperback) | BR350.B9 (ebook)

01/20/22

To the memory of William Peter Stephens
Superb Bullinger scholar and wonderful Christian person

To all the readers of this book
May they learn appreciatively from Heinrich Bullinger
about Christian faith and life

CONTENTS

Foreword by Emidio Campi • ix

Preface • xix

Acknowledgments • xxiii

Introduction • xxv

1 Heinrich Bullinger's Life • 1

2 Holy Scripture • 13

3 God • 32

4 Christ • 44

5 Holy Spirit • 57

6 Predestination and Covenant • 75

7 Sin and Salvation • 92

8 Church and Ministry • 105

9 Word and Sacraments • 123

10 The State and Last Things • 138

11 The Abiding Significance of Heinrich Bullinger • 152

Selected Bibliography • 161

FOREWORD

OVER THE LAST THREE decades research on the Zurich Reformation has increasingly turned to the period immediately before and after the frantic years of the 1520s. Without in any way downplaying the fundamental significance of the early phase of the Reformation, recent studies show that between 1531 and 1575 many rough attempts at reform matured into functional institutions, and at same time notable signs of renewal appeared that consolidated and strengthened the influential role of the church of Zurich in the context of the Confederation and at the European level throughout the sixteenth century and beyond. The principal driving force behind the process was Heinrich Bullinger (1504–75), undisputedly the second Zurich reformer and the adviser to most Reformed churches of Europe.[1]

For forty-four years, he served as *Antistes* (Head pastor) of the Zurich church, which he prudently guided through the perils of a turbulent age, while at the same time developing an astonishingly intensive activity as preacher.

---

1. Amy Nelson Burnett and Emidio Campi (eds), *A Companion to the Swiss the Swiss Reformation* (Leiden: Brill, 2016), 59–125; Emidio Campi, "From 'Zwinglian' to 'Swiss' Reformation. What's in a Name?" in Adriane Albisser, Peter Opitz (eds), *Die Zürcher Reformation in Europa: Beiträge der Tagung des Instituts für schweizerische Reformationsgeschichte 2019* (Zurich: TVZ, 2021), 15–43.

Foreword

In addition to his obligations as chief minister, Bullinger built up a partly newly conceived school system, and with his energetic support, the *Prophezei*, founded 1525 by Zwingli for the training of the clergy, developed into the *Schola Tigurina*, a theological institution that played a leading role within the Reformed world. Also Zurich's concrete relief actions in the sixteenth century to aid hard-pressed coreligionists were mainly inspired by Bullinger's deep concern for their fate.

It must be noted that during his tenure Bullinger also became entangled in a web of inner contradictions. Despite holding a somewhat more sensible attitude towards the Jews or the Turks than most of the reformers, one can only deplore the alacrity with which he combated them in his writings and sermons. Further, his acrimonious disputes with the religious dissidents cast a long shadow over his relative irenicism. Critical, from today's viewpoint, was Bullinger's ambiguous acquiescence in the burning of Servetus as a heretic in Geneva, the polemic campaign against Caspar Schwenckfeld, the intolerant dealing with Bernardino Ochino, and above all his relentless fight against the Anabaptists. On the whole, however, Bullinger as leader of the Zurich church was more successful than his predecessor in preserving the precarious balance of power between church and state—avoiding both perilous confusion and absolute separation.

Bullinger's *œuvre* as theologian and scholar can be easily seen from his impressive literary production, which includes more than 130 printed works, whose dissemination throughout Europe was extremely high for his time. Besides polemic treatises and pastoral and doctrinal writings spanning nearly the whole spectrum of Christian theology, he was the author of expanded commentaries on all of the New Testament books, on Genesis, Jeremiah, Daniel, and Isaiah. By far his most comprehensive theological work was the *Sermonum Decades quinque,* which alongside John Calvin's *Institutes* and Peter Martyr Vermigli's *Loci communes* is a classic of the early Reformed Protestantism. The title comes from the classification of the work into five groups of ten sermons each, hence "decades". The fact that the material is presented in the form of fifty teaching sermons, probably delivered to the pastors of the city, reveals Bullinger's prominent quality as theologian. Theology does not have an essentially different task than a sermon; it serves to orient the practical life of believers providing a new alternative vision of God's purposes for church and society. Bullinger is also the author of the Second Helvetic Confession (1566), formally accepted as symbolic book by numerous Reformed churches, and a storehouse from which later framers of Reformed confessions have copiously drawn.

Bullinger contributed much more than is often recognized to the shaping of Reformed Protestantism. There is a considerable body of evidence that during forty-four years he tried—not always with success—to strengthen the connections between Zurich, Berne, and Basel, as well as with the other Protestant cantons, especially Grisons, and that the close relationship with Geneva formed a constant in his theological and church-political efforts. Moreover, he had a significant impact on ecclesiastical politics in numerous territories of the Holy Roman Empire, England, France, Poland, and Lithuania. Nothing else makes plainer the stunning geographic breadth of Bullinger's influence than his immense correspondence, which comprises about twelve thousand letters, of which about two thousand are written by him and the others come from a multitude of correspondents. Among them we find such prominent church leaders, princes, military commanders, scholars, and reformers as Luther, Melanchthon, Calvin, Bucer, Cranmer, King Edward VI, King Sigismund II of Poland, Philip of Hesse, Gaspard de Coligny, Thomas Erastus, Bonifacius Amerbach, and many more, as well as little-known pastors from the countryside, women, refugees, students.

Finally, it is worth mentioning that Bullinger—besides his varied activities—had a life-long and intensive interest in historical studies. Indeed, he was a historian of recognized format, who left behind an impressive body of writings, mostly *still unpublished* and currently under study. They were not limited to the history of the church, such as the renowned *History of the Reformation*. The main was made up of profane historical works, such as the comprehensive accounts of the Swiss Confederation and the history of the Zurich city.[2]

In short, the conclusion that can be drawn from recent research is the following: Bullinger was able to preserve Zwingli's legacy, adapting some of his path-breaking insights to the changing theological, ecclesiastical, and political circumstances, and establishing Zurich as a center of international Protestantism.

The high esteem in which Heinrich Bullinger is held by more recent research is regrettably out of proportion to the attention that his life and work receive in textbooks, where his importance in the history of the Reformation is assured, but at the same time, with few exceptions, also checked off without due in-depth consideration. The problem with the traditional print model of textbooks is that it is often slow in keeping up with research findings and usually does

---

2. Heinrich Bullinger, *Werke, Historische Schriften* 1: *Tigurinerchronik*, edited by Hans Ulrich Bächtold, 3 vols. (Zurich: TVZ 2018); Christian Moser, *Die Dignität des Ereignisses. Studien zu Heinrich Bullingers Reformationsgeschichtsschreibung*, 2 vols. (Leiden: Brill, 2012).

not encourage deep learning from source material. This is where the present book comes in. As concise account of central themes of Heinrich Bullinger's thought drawn from his main works, the *Decades* and the Second Helvetic Confession, it can be used in schools, parishes, undergraduate or graduate classrooms to supplement other resources in order to achieve a deeper knowledge of the reformer.

There is no need to discuss here the content of each of the 10 chapters. Let me give just a few examples to illustrate why it is so. Textbooks usually label Bullinger's eucharistic theology as a form of "late Zwinglanism". But if one reads the pages of this book dedicated to the topic, with lengthy quotations drawn from Bullingers works, one will find out that, despite profound affinity, his eucharistic theology differed from that of Zwingli already in its premise. Zwingli began by advocating a symbolic view of the sacrament, hence underlying the memorial and corporate aspect of the meal, and then from 1529 increasingly emphasized the character of gift and the spiritual presence of Christ. Bullinger from the beginning went beyond a purely symbolic understanding of the sacraments and asserted the connection between sign and reality.[3] Based on his steadfast conviction of the covenantal unity of both Testaments, he regarded the Passover meal and the Lord's Supper as signs and tokens of the "one and eternal covenant" between God and humanity. He saw, therefore, the sacraments not as empty symbols, but as an illustration of the saving grace.

However, Bullinger did not simply stiffen in the acquired position. Rather the alarming situation of Protestantism in central Europe after the Augsburg Interim, as well as the intensive exchange of ideas with Calvin, led him to refine further the doctrine of sacraments as it appears in

3. Heinrich Bullinger, "De sacrifitio missae (1524)," in: HBTW 2, 39–40; "De institutione eucharistiae (1525)," in: HBTW 2, 89–100.

the *Consensus Tigurinus* of 1549.[4] No efforts were spared by either side to produce a joint statement: they exchanged many letters and drafts of solutions and met three times for consultations in Zurich, where Guillaume Farel also helped. It is fainéant to discuss whether the Agreement of Zurich echoes more Calvinian or Bullingerian theology, although an in-depth treatment of Calvin's eucharistic theology not only asserts "Calvin's submission to Zurich in 1549" but also concludes that "Bullingerizing accents were to go on resounding after 1549, in a similar quantity as the anti-Zwinglian statements before 1549."[5] The real point is that what seemed to its contemporaries a text with a host of qualifications and ambiguities ranking a little below Luther and a little above Zwingli, and therefore fundamentally divisive, became an indispensable reference document for the Reformed doctrine of the Lord's Supper, which found its mature expression in the Heidelberg Catechism and the Second Helvetic Confession. Moreover, it was a seed of hope that anticipated the Leunberg Concord of 1973, the intra-Protestant agreement that overcame the strife between Lutherans and Reformed over the Lord's Supper and enabled Protestant churches to enter into table fellowship.

Was Bullinger a double predestinarian? (Chapter 6.) Most textbooks, if they tackle the question at all, answer with a resolute: No. In the *Decades,* however, the reformer writes: "The predestination is the eternal decree of God, whereby he hath ordained either to save or destroy men;

---

4. *Reformation Debates over the Lord's Supper (1536–1560): Sources and Impact of the Consensus Tigurinus.* Special Issue of *Reformation & Renaissance Review* 18 (2016), edited by Emidio Campi and Torrance Kirby.

5. Wim Janse, "Calvin's Eucharistic Theology: Three Dogma-Historical Observations," in Herman J. Selderhuis (ed.), *Calvinus sacrarum literarum interpres : papers of the International Congress on Calvin Research* (Göttingen: V&R, 2008), 27–69

Foreword

a most certain end of life and death being appointed unto them" (Dec. 4, 4). He nevertheless clearly rejects any speculative train of thought as well as any hint of determinism, and he focuses on the universality of God's saving grace in Christ. More precisely: he emphasizes both the universality of salvation and the culpability of the reprobate for their ultimate condemnation. Thus, beyond the visible pastoral concern it emerges a consolatory message for the believers: the core of predestination is the election in Christ; decisive for the eternal election or reprobation is the communion with Christ, which is realized in faith. In other words, for Bullinger the central matter in eternal election or reprobation is not "God's eternal decree," but rather the communion with Christ realized through faith.

The second part of the chapter 6 helps in clarifying the notion of "covenant" and thus enables readers to evaluate the fallacy of the opaque characterization of Bullinger as the "father of covenant theology", in the sense of a contract, a mutual agreement between God and human beings. It shows that Bullinger in his early writing uses the concept in connection with the sacraments. Subsequently, in the *Decades*, the concept of covenant reaches beyond an exposition of the sacraments and describes the fundamental situation where humans encounter God and are received by his mercy. The theme reaches its full development when Bullinger brings the Christological character of the covenant to the fore—namely in the completed redemption in Christ and the consequent renewal of humanity. No wonder that Gottfried W. Locher calls the rediscovery of the biblical concept of covenant by Zwingli, Ecolampadius, and Bullinger "the most important contribution to the Reformation."[6]

---

6. Gottfried W. Locher, *Zwingli's Thought: New Perspectives* (Leiden: Brill, 1981), 29.

An equally original theological profile shows Bullinger's treatment of the controversial doctrine of justification. Fundamental to Bullinger's understanding of justification is the imputation of Christ's alien righteousness. It is through Christ's righteousness (and not through our own works) that we come to God, and his righteousness becomes ours. For Bullinger, however, righteousness is never simply imputed. It is also imparted. Clearly under the impression of the changed theological landscape after the first session of the Council of Trent and in contrast to Luther's predominant accentuation of justification, Bullinger reiterates that the righteousness of Christ bestowed upon us is never simply an atonement for our sins, it is the initial and continuing source of a new life in pneumatological communion with Christ, that is the sanctification. Justification and sanctification are distinct but interrelated. He can describe the justification both as adoption to be children of God (*adoptio*) as well as a vivifying power, which enables a new life in the Spirit (*vivificatio*).[7] Thus Bullinger's decisive theological achievement becomes clear: while emphasizing God's sole activity and human passivity in the process of justification, he declares even more than the German reformer the sanctification as an essential consequence of God's love for humanity.

The authors of the book point out that here is an important clue that helps to illuminate Bullinger's understanding of justification. Since 1523 he had the words from Matthew 17:5 on the title page of almost all his printed works: "This is my beloved Son, in whom I am reconciled. Listen to him!" He intentionally translates the original Greek verb *eudokeo* with *versoehnen*, "to be reconciled," and the imperative *akouete* with *ihm seid gehoerig*, which means both "to be attentive," and "to obey." The contribution this

---

7. Bullinger, *Decades* 1,6, p. 106–7.

peculiar interpretation makes, emphasizing the necessity both for hearing the word of Christ as well as for the obedience of the faith, is in any case plain—for Bullinger, Christ's work aims at the ethical renewing of human life. Justifying righteousness attained solely through faith is always accompanied by sanctifying righteousness and does not obviate the responsibility of Christians to strive after the new life in Christ. This understanding of the ethical renewal of Christian life out of grace, whose importance in Bullinger's thought can hardly be exaggerated, constitute the center of his soteriology, and may well have oriented his efforts to resolve disputes among the Reformation churches, keeping the way open for dialogue.

The book is concerned for the most part with extolling Bullinger's theological thought. But another positive feature of this book is that the authors do not show the proverbial *fois du charbonnier*. They do not minimize the hard confrontation of the reformer with the Anabaptist and other opponents, but after offering readers a survey of the remarks of the "inveterate foe"—as they label Bullinger—against the dissenters, they consider the biblical and theological reasons of the latter, in a manner more sympathetic.

Understandably, the book cannot dispel all common misconceptions of Bullinger, neither tackle all aspects of his thought. Nonetheless, it is a unique glimpse into the life and thought of Bullinger and an excellent primary source. I heartily recommend it to scholars and students interested in history of the Zurich Reformation, or the Reformed Churches.

Emidio Campi

PREFACE

It has been our pleasure to write this book on Heinrich Bullinger together.

Jim West and Don McKim are friends through the internet and phone calls. Though we have not met in person—writing this book during the COVID-19 pandemic did not easily permit this possibility—we have read each other's books through the years. We both share a passion for sixteenth-century Reformation studies including the theology of the Protestant reformers. When Jim suggested to Don that we do a book together, Don readily agreed and this book on Bullinger was born.

We agreed we both wanted to do what we believe has not been done in the English language before: present a book on Heinrich Bullinger that introduces persons without technical theological backgrounds to the basics of Bullinger's life (albeit briefly) and theology. For those persons who may be curious; as well as for pastors who may have had a brief brush with Bullinger while in seminary; and those laypersons in churches who are interested to know about an important theologian—what he believed and what significance Bullinger may have for their lives of Christian faith today—we wrote this book. There are technical studies of Bullinger's theology for scholars. But we wanted to introduce Heinrich Bullinger to those for whom technical studies are not especially helpful.

We greatly enjoyed working on this book together and hope it will be a helpful resource. We wanted Bullinger to speak for himself with our comments being a guide to Bullinger's contexts, meanings, and the importance of what he wrote.

Jim would like to thank Don for his collegiality, good humor, encouragement, and wisdom. Jim also thanks his wife Doris and daughter Rachel, who have put up with his scholarly interests for many decades and have never shown the slightest sign of disinterest.

Don would like to thank Jim for this wonderful opportunity to work together and all his kindnesses and great insights. Don also thanks LindaJo, his loving wife, and their sons and families: Stephen and Caroline and their children, Maddie, Annie, Jack, and Ford; and Karl and Lauren. They bring greatest joys to life.

It, further, would not be proper for us to forget to thank Robin Parry of Cascade Books. Robin is one of the kindest persons in publishing and his work is extraordinary. We are most grateful for his support of this project and his friendship.

This book is dedicated to the memory our friend and colleague William Peter Stephens, who though now in Glory would, we think, be extremely pleased to know that Bullinger is getting more 'press' in the English-speaking world than he has had in a century. We also dedicate it to the readers to come. We pray Almighty God will be as important to them as he was to Bullinger, and that Bullinger can serve as their very faithful guide to a deeper Christian life.

Finally, we offer this book on Heinrich Bullinger in gratitude for his life, his theology, and his faith. On the title page of all Bullinger's printed works, this biblical text from the Gospel of Matthew's account of the transfiguration of Christ was quoted: "This is my beloved Son in whom I am reconciled. Listen to him!" (Matt 17:5). We affirm what Bullinger said of Jesus Christ:

> God the heavenly Father has given his only Son Jesus Christ as the only, and eternal advocate, mediator, defender and protector. To the Father he is the greatest, most beloved, most worthy and most pleasing. Nothing is lacking in him which a true mediator and advocate should be. He is lord of all, is friendly (*fruntlich*) and merciful to all poor sinners, he invites all to himself and promises them all truth and love.[1]

Let us listen to him!

Jim West, Petros, Tennessee
Donald K. McKim, Germantown, Tennessee
Advent, 2021

---

1. Cited in Bruce Gordon, "Bullinger's Vernacular Writings: Spirituality and the Christian Life," in Bruce Gordon and Emidio Campi, ed., *Architect of Reformation: An Introduction to Heinrich Bullinger 1504–1575*, Rpt. (Eugene, OR: Wipf and Stock Publishers, 2019), 117.

ACKNOWLEDGMENTS

Material from Arthur C. Cochrane, ed., *Reformed Confessions of the Sixteenth Century*; new introduction by Jack Rogers (Louisville, KY: Westminster John Knox, 2003). Used by kind permission of Westminster John Knox Press (www.wjkbooks.com).

INTRODUCTION

Welcome to *Heinrich Bullinger!*

We are delighted to present this book as a "gateway to Bullinger." Our hope is to introduce the theological thought of one of the greatest, yet lesser known, sixteenth-century Protestant reformers. Bullinger was a theologian and pastor who plumbed the depths of Scripture and provided insights that helped guide Protestant churches and Christian believers during his lifetime and beyond. And though more people today have heard of John Calvin, in Bullinger's day he was far more 'famous' and influential.

Heinrich Bullinger (1504–75) was the successor of Huldrych Zwingli (1484–1531) as chief pastor of the church in Zurich and led that church for nearly fifty years. Bullinger wrote a massive amount on a wide variety of topics. Regrettably, not many of his works have been translated into English. Indeed, the main English-languages sources of Bullinger's work are the nineteenth-century translations of his *Decades*—fifty (long!) sermons on theological themes; and his *The Second Helvetic Confession* (1566), which became one of the most important confessions of faith among Protestants.

As noted above, while Bullinger was known and respected across Europe in his day, he is barely known today by pastors and in churches. Zwingli is sometimes called "the forgotten reformer of the sixteenth century." The names of Martin Luther and John Calvin are most well-known. But, the name "Heinrich Bullinger" is even less well-known than Zwingli's. Here, we hope to show that Bullinger's theology was important for the Protestant movement; and also, that his work has meaning and significance for Christians today. In one sense, we are asking the question asked in the book of Ezekiel: "Can these bones live?" (Ezek 37:3). Can the theology of a pastor in Zurich, Switzerland in the sixteenth century, the son of a priest, take on importance for Christians here and now, in the twenty-first century? We believe the answer is "Yes!"—the theology of Heinrich Bullinger can provide biblical and theological insights that can focus and shape our beliefs and also provide directions for our lives and our faith today.

We hope this book will be a "gateway" to Bullinger. We have written it to introduce the life and theology of this Reformation pastor to those without a specialized background in historical theology. We anticipate pastors and lay persons in churches will be readers who will learn of Bullinger for the first time or will gain clarity into whatever they may previously have known about the Zurich reformer. We want to present Bullinger's theology in a fresh and accessible way. This is not a "technical" theological book, though it will deal with topics that have been the subject of deep theological discussions in the past. Footnotes have been kept to an absolute minimum (though some readers may still think there are too many). We want to let Bullinger speak in his own voice as much as possible while we present the key features of his theology and its importance for us now.

Our approach will be to look at the main theological themes in Bullinger's thought, arranged as theological doctrines. These present Bullinger's understandings of what

Introduction

each topic means for Christian faith and life. At points, Bullinger presented understandings that were at variance with the thought of other Protestant reformers. We try to note when this happened. Bullinger worked with the theological *loci*—the topics (literally "places") of Christian theology. But his theology was not explicitly "systematic." As one scholar noted, Bullinger "preferred the dynamic relationship between the individual and the Word."[1] Bullinger's theology is marked by a lively engagement with Scripture as the Word of God. He believed the task of biblical interpretation was at the center of the church's theological life. The Holy Spirit leads and guides our interpretation of Scripture as we use the best tools available for understanding biblical texts. So, readers of the Bible can have a "dynamic relationship" with the Word of God.

This is a basic reality that can shape our beliefs and understandings and our ways of living. Reading Bullinger's theology brings us directly in touch with scriptural interpretations and their meanings for what the church believes—and what we can believe. Bullinger had full confidence that in our encounter with Scripture, in our efforts to understand the meanings of biblical texts, and, through the work of the Holy Spirit, our ability to receive the messages God intends for us to know. We can trust God; and we can believe God will act in our lives according to God's providence and loving good will for us. This makes Scripture reading and theological understanding dynamic and life-changing!

We trust this book will present Bullinger's theological insights with clarity and we hope those insights will energize those who will find Bullinger's theology a solid basis for faithful discipleship in today's world.

---

1. Bruce Gordon, "Introduction" in Gordon and Campi, eds., *Architect of Reformation*, 29.

1

HEINRICH BULLINGER'S LIFE[1]

AT THE AGE OF seventy-one, Heinrich Bullinger breathed his last as a seizure racked his body and rendered him lifeless. He had fallen victim to seizures several times over the last months of his life, with an extraordinarily powerful one striking him on May 24, 1575 and its ill effects lingered until 17 September, when death took him.

---

1. To borrow a phrase from Thomas Harding in his "Life of Bullinger" from volume 5 of the English edition of the *Decades*—"the following abstract of Bullinger's life has been compiled from a Diary of Bullinger's, in the Library of Zurich (Acta Eccles. Mscr. F. 106); from a memoir of Bullinger, in the 1st volume of Miscell. Tigur. part 2; from the biographies of Simler, Melchior Adam, and Pastor Hess; and from D'Aubigne's History of the Reformation, (Books viii. xi. xv. xvi.), where much use has been made of Bullinger's own 'Chronick.'" (Harding, *Decades* 5:vii). If readers add Harding to that venerable list of sources drawn upon, he or she will know from whence the details of Bullinger's life spring. Though what follows is greatly expanded, chiefly on the basis of *Bullinger's Correspondence*, available at http://teoirgsed.uzh.ch/.

BULLINGER'S EARLY LIFE

Bullinger's life had commenced seventy-one years earlier, on July 18, 1504, in the beautiful little town of Bremgarten. His father, a priest, had already fathered four children with his papally approved wife Anna. Priestly celibacy, though the official stance of the Roman Catholic Church for centuries, was widely ignored and many priests had mistresses, wives, or concubines. Or they simply made use of the prostitutes who were widely available in sixteenth-century Europe. Hardly any priests were actually celibate. Heinrich's father, Heinrich, was simply one priest among many who had families.

Heinrich's home life was typical. He experienced the usual trials of childhood. He was injured while walking along the street one day when he fell and a whistle he was carrying was shoved into his neck. His family was touched by the plague. He was nearly abducted by a beggar, to who knows what end or purpose. He was, by all accounts (or the few accounts we actually possess, and these mostly based on his diary), a normal child in a normal family from a normal home in a normal town. That status as "average" would be overturned in 1531 and thereafter when he would take charge of the church in Zurich.

Before arriving in Zurich, though, Bullinger had to attend school. At the age of five he started his schooling in Bremgarten. He continued there until he arrived at the ripe old age of twelve years, when he was sent off, on June 11, 1516, to the grammar school at Emmerich on the Rhine. This was no short distance or easy journey and it would have taken the twelve-year-old boy 614 kilometers to the north, passing through the territories of Strasbourg, Koblenz, Bonn, Cologne, and Essen, arriving on the border of the Netherlands and taking up residence at his new home. This was Bullinger's first exposure to the world beyond his native Switzerland and portended his extensive international contacts in later life.

Bullinger remained at Emmerich for three years. There he became expert in Latin. Because his financial circumstances were underwhelming, he had to earn money by going from house to house, where he would sing and kind souls would give him cash for his troubles. This was not a strategy of survival for Bullinger alone though. Many students across Germany did the same, including none less than Martin Luther himself off to the east.

Heinrich's father Heinrich could have sent more funding in support of his son, but chose not to do so. The elder Heinrich wished to teach his son a valuable lesson: concern for the poor. And he believed that the best way to do this was to ensure his own son's poverty. What better way, he reasoned, to teach compassion than to force one's child to find it necessary to be on the receiving end of the compassion of others.

Young Heinrich's goal as he pursued his education at Emmerich was to eventually enter the order of the Carthusians. This order of Catholic Monks was famously strict; indeed, it was deemed the strictest of all the monastic orders. Founded in 1084 by Bruno of Cologne and made up of both nuns and monks, the order was primarily engaged in performing acts of charity for the very poor. Heinrich's personality as a teen, casting his gaze at a monastic order that was primarily known for its acts of compassion, perfectly foreshadows the adult he would become. His life's trajectory was set. He would become one of the most influential Reformers concerning "poor relief" and he later authored several treatises as the Antistes of the Zurich church concerning how the poor in the city should be treated.

MINISTRY BEFORE THE CALL TO ZURICH

Emmerich was Bullinger's home until July 8, 1519, when he moved to Cologne and commenced studies there at the university. The 125-kilometer journey to the south would have taken approximately twenty-six hours of foot travel, or about three to four days journey. The university there had a long and important history, it being the sixth university in Central Europe that had ever been founded (in 1388), and the fourth established by the Holy Roman Emperor (after Prague, 1348, Vienna, 1365, and Heidelberg, 1386).

Interestingly, it was while Bullinger the younger was at Cologne that Bullinger the elder, back in Bremgarten, like Luther, too, was engaged in conflict with the selling of indulgences.

As a student in Cologne, Bullinger focused his attention on the works of Peter Lombard and Gratian, the two major theologians of the Middle Ages and still important academically in the sixteenth century. Curiously it was with the study of the two Roman Catholic academic icons that Bullinger began to slowly but surely move away from the papacy. It seems that with contact with Lombard and Gratian he was introduced to the church fathers, and with that introduction his appetite was whet for more.

Later in life this interest in the fathers would bear fruit in, for instance, his sermons found in the famous *Decades*. Treating repentance, Bullinger writes:

> And as diversely too is repentance defined of the ecclesiastical writers: howbeit all agree that it is a conversion or turning to the Lord, and an alteration of the former life and opinion. We therefore do say, that repentance is an unfeigned turning to God, whereby we, being of a sincere fear of God once humbled, do acknowledge our sins,

and so, by mortifying our old man, are afresh renewed by the Spirit of God.[2]

The church fathers were fodder for Bullinger's ever-growing theological awareness from his days at the University of Cologne.

But the fathers weren't the only things that Bullinger was consuming at the university. He also there became acquainted with the early works of Luther and Melanchthon. And he also obtained a copy of the New Testament of Erasmus and spent a good deal of his time reading through it, with the assistance of Jerome's Commentaries.

As was the case with Zwingli and Luther as well as with Calvin, the "conversion" of Bullinger to an "evangelical" (in the sixteenth-century meaning of the word) faith was a progressive, slow, measured, steady departure rather than a sudden, dramatic, fiery break.

Bullinger finished his studies at Cologne in 1522, receiving there the Bachelor's Degree in October of 1522 and the Master's Degree in 1522. Then he returned home to Bremgarten, where he would remain occupied in personal studies for the next year.

In 1523 a vacancy came open at the Cistercian Abbey of Kappel-am-Albis, a lovely village in the environs of Zurich, four hours walk to the South, a mere twenty kilometers away, situated in the canton of Zug. It was the home of the battlefield where both the First Kappel War of 1529 and the Second Kappel War of 1531 would be waged between Catholics and Reformed and where, on October 11, 1531, Zwingli would die while serving as chaplain to the Zurich troops.

But in 1523 none of that was on the horizon and the Abbey was a peaceful, lovely place where Bullinger had both

2. Bullinger, *Decades*, 4:56–57.

the freedom and the inspiration to continue his studies of the fathers and the Bible. At Kappel-am-Albis Bullinger's responsibility was to teach the monks and other students and to do so without any dogmatic constraints. He was free, in short, to teach the truth. This he was happy to do and the deal was made on January 17, 1523.

The six years that Bullinger spent at Kappel-am-Albis were personally fulfilling and extremely productive. He composed over fifty different tracts, some of which would later find a place in his published works. It was during these years that Bullinger made the acquaintance of both Huldrych Zwingli and Leo Jud of Zurich. Bullinger was so taken with Zwingli's teachings, especially on the Eucharist, that he took a leave of absence from the Abbey and spent five months in Zurich attending Zwingli's lectures at the *Prophezei* and deepening his understanding of both the Greek and Hebrew Scriptures. It was also during this period that Bullinger began corresponding with theologians and pastors all across Europe. The first preserved letter in our possession dates to June 24, 1524 and the last dates to the year of his death. Over the decades, Bullinger wrote two thousand letters and he was the recipient of ten thousand letters.

> Geographically, the network of this correspondence stretches from Scotland to Belarus and from Denmark to Italy. All in all, there are more than 1,100 correspondents involved, originating from many different social classes: from kings, politicians and scholars to workmen with quite rudimentary literacy skills. Almost all of the letters were written in Latin (80%) and Early Modern German (20%), except occasional letters composed in French, Italian or Greek.[3]

3. http://teoirgsed.uzh.ch/, accessed 21 September, 2020.

At present, only the letters through March 1547 have been published. Numerous volumes remain to be edited.

By December 1527, Bullinger was viewed as of such significance to the Zurich magistrates that they deputized him to attend the Conference at Berne in 1528 and to accompany Zwingli to it. When he returned to Kappel-am-Albis he was called to the pastoral office and would preach his first sermon on June 21, 1528. He would preach his last sermon decades later in 1575.

Bullinger was a famously long-winded preacher. He was known to regularly preach for up to two hours and his audiences were frequently well worn out by the time the service was over. In spite of that, the church was regularly full.

Bullinger's first pastoral calling was back to his home town of Bremgarten. There he preached, beginning on June 1, 1529, the doctrines and teachings of the Reformation. On August 17, 1529 at the little village church of Birmenstorf near Bremgarten, he was married to a former nun, Anne Adlischweiler of Zurich. The two years spent at Bremgarten as the pastor of the good people there were some of the happiest of Bullinger's life. The stresses to follow when he would assume the pastorate of the Great Minster in Zurich and the several illnesses those stresses would cause were years away. Life in Bremgarten was good.

Things turned much darker in October 1531 when the Reformed were soundly defeated by the Catholic cantons at the Second Battle of Kappel-am-Albis. The death of Huldrych Zwingli sent shock waves through the cantons, and it looked to many as though the reforming efforts of that

---

Reinhard Bodenmann, the chief editor of the Bullinger correspondence, has privately communicated that the letters of Bullinger are an incredibly rich source of information for his life and thought. Many of Bullinger's letters will be the source of much of what follows.

man would end with his death. However, fortunately, the stressful tensions and uncertainties of the times resulted in migrations from surrounding lands to Zurich where those of reforming mindsets, those aligned theologically with Zwingli, would go for refuge. Among them was Heinrich Bullinger, along with his family and his parents.

Through what can only be described as the moving of Providence, after settling in the city on November 21, a few weeks later, on December 9, after declining pastorates in both Basel and Berne, Bullinger was appointed by the senate of Zurich to Zwingli's vacancy as the Cathedral pastor. There he would remain until his death in 1575. His ministry in Zurich spanned a remarkable forty-four years.

THE ZURICH YEARS

Bullinger's ministry for the first seven years, from 1531 to 1538, saw him preaching at least once every day of the week and twice a day on many occasions. Besides his duties in the pulpit, he wrote a large number of booklets covering every subject from the meaning of the "prophetic office" to exegeses of Hebrews, the Letter to the Romans, and the Epistles of John. This is not to mention polemical tractates responding to various Catholic authors who were attempting to bring the Reform into disrepute. Most of these works were in Latin, but a few were written in German, and intended for the larger populace. One of the more engaging of these, published in 1535, was concerning the proper treatment of the sick and dying, titled "*Bericht der Krancken : wie man by den krancken und sterbenden Menschen handeln, ouch wie sich ein yeder inn siner Kranckheit schicken unnd zum sterben rüsten sölle / kurtzer unnd einfallter Bericht Heinrychen Bullingers.*" The English title is "*Report on the sick: how to deal with sick and dying people, also how each of them conduct themselves in their sickness and should prepare for death / a brief and succinct report, by Heinrich Bullinger."* Titles in the sixteenth century tended to be quite long!

Regrettably, this text has never been translated into English. And aside from *The Decades*, a series of sermons Bullinger preached, neither has much else that flowed from his productive pen. Along with all of these tasks, the first seven years of Bullinger's pastorate in Zurich also saw him exchanging letters with many of the most important theologians of his day. These included Berchtold Haller, Wolfgang Capito, Leo Jud, Erasmus Ritter, and Wolfgang Joner. He was also sought out by various city leaders in the Reformed cantons for theological advice. In short, Bullinger was the most important Reformed theologian of the day, far eclipsing the barely known John Calvin. Indeed, during the sixteenth century, while he lived, Bullinger's authority always exceeded that of Calvin's. During the trial of Servetus, Calvin consulted with Bullinger to obtain his advice, and during the sometimes-tense negotiations over a common Reformed confession, it was Bullinger's views that prevailed, not Calvin's.

Bullinger, in short, was to become the most important Reformed thinker of the sixteenth century, and everyone wanted his input and advice and guidance. This is a truly remarkable fact, given that today he is virtually unknown outside of specialist circles.

In 1536, just five short years after Zwingli's untimely death, the senate of Zurich appointed both Bullinger and Leo Jud to attend a conference in Basel where a Reformed confession was being decided upon. The result was The First Helvetic Confession, published that same year. It was there that Bullinger and Calvin first met, and where they struck up a lifelong friendship. It was also in that same year that Bullinger's fame reached England and from thence he began to receive into his home in Zurich English theologians seeking further guidance regarding the Reformed faith.

In 1541 tragedy struck the Bullinger family with the passing of his mother during an outbreak of the plague. Her death, on August 16, left an indelible mark on Bullinger's thinking and his letter to Oswald Myconius on August 31 describes his sadness at her loss.[4] And Bullinger suffered another serious loss when one of his children died on September 30, and just a few months later, in 1542, on June 19, his colleague and dear friend Leo Jud died.

Bullinger continued to occupy himself with the labors of his office and with the tasks of a renowned and much sought-after theologian. Visitors from England continued to arrive and they found in Bullinger's house a warm welcome. So too did visitors from Geneva—namely, Calvin and Farel, who in 1549 met with Bullinger at his home in Zurich to hash out the "Zurich Consensus," one of the most important Reformed documents related to the understanding of the Lord's Supper, a long contentious issue indeed. The agreement of Zurich and Geneva on this matter meant that Calvin and Bullinger had achieved what Luther and Zwingli were unable to accomplish.

The consequence of this was not peace throughout Europe, though, as the papacy then condemned Bullinger and all his writings. Bullinger may have found himself in the crosshairs of papal rage, but he was, and continued to be, the most sought-after theologian in Europe, especially by the English.

The closing decades of Bullinger's life, from 1556 onwards, were riddled with conflict and controversy. His letters from that period are a parade of problematic persons who disputed with Bullinger concerning every conceivable

4. "Bullinger an Oswald Myconius," *Briefwechsel*, 11:302.

theological issue from the Lord's Supper to clerical practice to provision for the poor to clerical ethics to the connection of the church to the power of the magistrates, along with numerous practical issues like marriage and divorce and the need for the people to be at worship on the Lord's Day. As well, tractates against the Anabaptists appeared along with guidance for schools and educational matters. Bullinger even penned booklets against the practice of black magic and his own history of the Reformation. In sum, Bullinger was a man occupied with every sort of concern imaginable and the intersection of those concerns and Christianity.

1564 was a particularly tragic year in the life of Bullinger. His beloved wife died that year. As did his second daughter. The next year, 1565, a mere decade before his own death, Bullinger lost two more of his children: his eldest daughter, who had married Huldrych Zwingli's son Huldrych, and his third daughter, the wife of Josiah Simler. They all, sadly, died of the plague.

In 1565, Bullinger fell ill from the plague, as Zwingli had before him, in 1519. But that was not the final injustice inflicted in that dreadful period, for it was in 1565 as well that Bullinger was afflicted with the kidney stones that would make his remaining decade of life in many ways utterly unbearable.

In spite of it all, Bullinger continued working, writing, preaching, praying, counseling, encouraging, cajoling, rejoicing, weeping, and living a profoundly Christian life. He did what could be done for his city and the surrounding countryside when, in 1569, an extremely severe famine struck the region, lasting until 1574. Indeed, beginning in the 1550s a series of famines brought incredible misery to the population of Europe, culminating, in the 1590s, with the most severe famine of them all, what has been called by researchers, a "super-famine."[5]

That same year, 1574, Bullinger's health swiftly deteriorated. The long-term effects of the plague combined with the kidney stones and now a very severe, crippling seizure would be the bell tolling the announcement of his final months. He made a moderate recovery, miraculously, from that seizure. But he suffered another, more crippling seizure on May 24, 1575. The effects of this seizure removed him from all active pursuits and at the end he was only able to compose a letter to be delivered when he died to the Zurich magistrates. At the age of seventy-one, after having served the Zurich church for forty-four years, he breathed his last on Wednesday, September 17. A very cold winter would descend on Europe that year. And a very heavy sadness draped itself over the city of Zurich at the passing of its amazingly important pastor, teacher, and theologian.

QUESTIONS FOR DISCUSSION

1. How do you think Bullinger's childhood and training influenced his thinking?

2. What are the ways in which his father being a priest affected Bullinger?

3. Who in Bullinger's life had the most impact on his theology?

---

5. Cf. Alfani, *Famine*, 1–10.

2

HOLY SCRIPTURE

Heinrich Bullinger, like other sixteenth-century Protestant reformers, saw the Bible as Holy Scripture, given to us to be a foundation for Christian faith. The Bible is God's Word. The Bible is God's divine revelation. The Bible tells us who God is and what God has done. This means Scripture is the authority for our understanding of God and the source for all the church's teachings. The ongoing work of the church is to interpret Scripture and to understand what God is calling the church to believe and do in the present time. It was to this work that Heinrich Bullinger devoted his life.

BULLINGER'S EARLY UNDERSTANDINGS OF SCRIPTURE

When Bullinger was studying at the University of Cologne debates broke out in 1520 about the teachings of Martin Luther (1483–1546). Were Luther's teachings in accord with the traditional teachings of the Roman Catholic Church?

Or, was Luther devising thoughts on his own without conveying what the Roman church taught and believed?

Bullinger was unfamiliar with church teachings and Luther's views. So, he began to study the church's views. Roman Catholic experts advised Bullinger to read the works of medieval church theologians—Peter Lombard and Gratian, a twelfth-century jurist who composed his *Decretals* in which he presented thousands of church teachings to provide a framework for the church's canon law. These sources pointed Bullinger back to the theologians of the early church.

Bullinger also read Luther. When he did, he found that Luther more clearly represented the teachings of the early church than did the medieval theologians. While medieval theologians cited the early church theologians, the early church theologians cited the Bible. They looked to *Scripture* as the basis for their theological views. So Bullinger got a copy of the New Testament. Reading Scripture led him to reject the teachings of the Roman Catholic Church. Bullinger also read the *Loci Communes*, a theological work by Luther's close associate Philip Melanchthon.

When Bullinger became a schoolmaster at the monastery in Kappel, Switzerland, he lectured on the Bible. He taught the Bible with simplicity and lectured on nearly all the books of the New Testament. Bullinger depended on early church theologians as well as the writings of Luther and Melanchthon for help in understanding biblical texts.

When Bullinger succeeded Huldrych Zwingli as the main teacher of Scripture in Zurich, a city that had become Protestant, Bullinger continued to teach the Bible in addition to preaching on biblical passages. Through many years, Bullinger published biblical commentaries and sermons. In his theological writings, Scripture is prominent. What was Bullinger's "last will and testament," which became the

Second Helvetic Confession (1566), begins with a discussion of Scripture. The Bible is the authoritative Word of God. The task of ordained ministers in the church—as well as laypersons living their day-to-day lives—was to interpret and understand what the Scriptures have to say about what God has revealed and how the people of God are to live.

THE AUTHORITY OF SCRIPTURE

Scripture Is the Word of God

Bullinger wrote about the nature and authority of Scripture at various points throughout his writings. In 1536, as Reformed churches in Switzerland were attempting to find common ground with Lutherans, Bullinger and other colleagues were charged with writing a confession of faith to express the common beliefs of Reformed churches. The First Helvetic Confession (1536) was the result. Its first article, "Concerning Holy Scripture" expressed beliefs Bullinger was to hold throughout his life. The Confession said:

> The holy, divine, Biblical Scripture, which is the Word of God inspired by the Holy Spirit and delivered to the world by the prophets and apostles, is the most ancient, most perfect and loftiest teaching and alone deals with everything that serves the true knowledge, love and honor of God, as well as true piety and the making of a godly, honest and blessed life.[1]

Scripture is said to be the "Word of God," which is "inspired by the Holy Spirit," given to us by human writers—"prophets and apostles." This phrase joins together the Old Testament and the New Testament as the Word of God.

---

1. Cochrane, ed., *Reformed Confessions*, 100.

Scripture originates with God. The Holy Spirit inspired biblical writers so they conveyed God's Word through their human words. Scripture gives perfect teaching and provide all things needed for "the true knowledge, love and honor of God and leads us to a "godly, honest and blessed life." Bullinger himself would expand on these understandings of the nature of Holy Scripture and its authority.

For Bullinger, Scripture has authority in itself. It does not need human confirmation. This was a controversial point between Protestants and Roman Catholics. The Roman church argued that Scripture gained its authority because the church recognized it as the Word of God and thus confers authority upon Scripture. Church traditions were seen as equal with Scripture in authority.

Bullinger argued Scripture existed before the church. In Scripture we have the living voice of God, heard by biblical figures such as Moses and the prophets. In later times, the apostles preached the gospel of Jesus Christ before it was written into what became the Scriptures. In both instances, God's "Word" in Scripture is older and greater than the church. God's Word is spoken (to the biblical writers) and later written. Whether oral or written, God's Word is prior to the (Roman Catholic, or any other) church and, in fact, it is God's Word that calls the church into being. Biblical writers—such as Moses and the apostles—were those to whom God spoke and through whom God spoke. So, their authority was from God, not from humans. The apostles were commissioned by Jesus to teach and preach. They were led by the Holy Spirit. We know this through Holy Scripture. As Bullinger argued, apostolic preaching gains authority from God. Through the Holy Spirit, biblical writers were inspired. Their teachings are authoritative because they are from God. These biblical writings contain all that is necessary for salvation.

Holy Scripture

In light of Roman Catholic teaching, Bullinger's main conflict throughout his life was between the authority of Scripture and the authority of the church. This was the primary concern of all the Protestant reformers during the sixteenth-century Reformation. The question of whether the church was prior to Scripture or Scripture prior to the church was this basic question of authority. Ultimately, Bullinger appealed to God as the author of Scripture so the Bible needs no human "validation" or confirmation from humans for its authority. The church *receives* the Scripture—as God's gift. It does not have to approve the Scriptures, or confirm the Scriptures, or commend the Scriptures. Church councils and church traditions, Bullinger would argue, have authority only insofar as their teachings and actions are based upon Scripture, which is the source of our knowledge of God and God's revelation to human beings. As Bullinger put it in the Second Helvetic Confession:

> We believe and confess the canonical Scriptures of the holy prophets and apostles of both Testaments to be the true Word of God, and to have sufficient authority of themselves, not of men. For God himself spoke to the fathers, prophets, apostles, and still speaks to us through the Holy Scriptures.[2]

The authority of Scripture is expressed in meaningful and significant ways. The Scriptures are the authoritative source through which we know God and also what to believe and how to live. As Bullinger put it in the first of his *Decades*—fifty sermons on the Christian faith: "all true and heavenly wisdom" comes from Scripture and is not "drawn, taught, or, last of all, soundly confirmed from elsewhere

---

2. Cochrane, ed., *Reformed Confessions*, 224.

than out of the word of God."³ The phrase "word of God" (Latin *verbum Dei*), Bullinger says, signifies "the virtue and power of God." Here, he notes, it signifies "the speech of God, and the revealing of God's will."⁴ This comes to us through the voice of Christ, the prophets, and the apostles. Afterwards, it was recorded in writings, "which are rightly called 'holy and divine Scriptures.'" Since Scripture shows the mind of the one from whom it comes, therefore, said Bullinger, the Bible proclaims God. In Bullinger's language: "the word doth shew the mind of him out of whom it cometh; therefore, the word of God doth make declaration of God."⁵

The Scriptures convey God and have authority because they declare God. They are the source for Christian belief and for knowing God's will—what God has done, and what God desires of us. Bullinger wrote in The Second Helvetic Confession: "In this Holy Scripture, the universal Church of Christ has the most complete exposition of all that pertains to a saving faith, and also to the framing of a life acceptable to God."⁶ Throughout this Confession, Bullinger blended the theological and ethical—what to believe and how to live. Biblical authority is living and active in the life of the church and in the lives of Christian believers. As Scripture is interpreted, new insights into God's truth and God's will can emerge; new directions and dimensions of ways to live as God wills can break forth as well. These new directions affect the lives of individuals as we listen to Scripture. For Bullinger and other Protestant reformers, Scripture also opened new ways to understand how to worship and be faithful to God's will for the church.

3. Bullinger, *Decades*, 1:36.
4. Bullinger, *Decades*, 1:37.
5. Bullinger, *Decades*, 1:37.
6. Cochrane, ed., *Reformed Confessions*, 224.

Holy Scripture

Bullinger went on to speak of the certainty we have in the Word of God since "God's word is truth" (see John 17:17). We are able to perceive God's word to us since God desires to speak to humanity in human voices. God's voice comes to us through human voices. God uses humans to convey the divine Word and will and message: in a voice easily understood by humans and that addresses humans "according to the speech usually spoken" among people.[7]

We see this, Bullinger points out, in scriptural descriptions of God speaking to biblical people: Adam and Eve, Noah, David, the prophets, and others. When God gave the law to the people of Israel at Sinai, the Scripture reads: "These words the LORD spoke with a loud voice to your whole assembly at the mountain, out of the fire, the cloud, and the thick darkness" (Deut 5:22). For Bullinger, the supreme example of God's using humans to communicate God's word is Jesus Christ. In Jesus Christ, "the Word became flesh and lived among us" (John 1:14). God spoke to human beings by becoming a human being. Jesus Christ, as the church has believed, is "fully God and fully human." By the power of the Holy Spirit, God continues to speak the divine Word to humans through the Scriptures. As with the Old Testament prophets, Bullinger notes: they

---

7. Bullinger, *Decades*, 1:38. This is recognized as God's "accommodation" to human capacity. John Calvin (1509–64) stressed this way of address between God and humans. God did not require humans to learn to speak "God language," (which is impossible!); God chose to speak to humanity in "human languages." Calvin wrote: "For who . . . does not understand that, as nurses commonly do with infants, God is wont in a measure to 'lisp' in speaking to us? Thus such forms of speaking do not so much express clearly what God is like as accommodate the knowledge of him to our slight capacity. To do this he must descend far beneath his loftiness." See *Institutes* I.13.1. Holy Scripture comes to us in human words, written by humans who lived in specific times and places. See Rogers and McKim, *Authority and Interpretation of the Bible*, 98–100.

were "inspired from God out of heaven by the Holy Spirit of God: for it is God, which, dwelling by his Spirit in the minds of the prophets, speaketh to us by their mouths."[8]

God speaks to us in the Scriptures through biblical writers. Bullinger did not comment extensively about the canon of Scripture, the books that are included in the Bible. He mentions the biblical books as containing "the very word of God, first of all declared of the fathers, of Christ himself, and the apostles by word of mouth; and after that also written into books by the prophets and apostles."[9] Bullinger, like other Protestant reformers—especially Martin Luther—believed the Bible was not "dark" and incomprehensible. Scripture is a bright light that can be interpreted and understood by God's people. God communicates the true and living Word of God through the Scriptures.[10] Together, "the word of God is the speech of God, that is to say, the revealing of his good will to mankind, which . . . he did open to those first, ancient, and most holy fathers; who again by tradition did faithfully deliver it to their posterity."[11] Through these writings—inspired by the Spirit of God—we now have "the word of God as it was preached and written"; and we learn "how to live well and holily [in holiness]."[12]

THE SUFFICIENCY OF SCRIPTURE

After he discussed the meaning of the "Word of God," Bullinger addressed in his second sermon why God's Word is

---

8. Bullinger, *Decades*, 1:50.
9. Bullinger, *Decades*, 1:54.
10. See Bullinger, *Decades*, 1:55.
11. Bullinger, *Decades*, 1:55.
12. Bullinger, *Decades*, 1:56.

revealed; in what ways it is to be heard; and the effects of the Word of God.

God is a God of all persons and nations "who desires everyone to be saved and to come to the knowledge of the truth" (1 Tim 2:4). Therefore, God has "for the benefit, life, and salvation" of all, "revealed his word, that so indeed there might be a rule and certain way to lead men by the path of justice into life everlasting."[13] This is the divine purpose of the Scriptures: to lead to eternal life—which comes through Jesus Christ. God's Word is revealed in Scripture to show how God relates to us humans and how God saves us through faith in Jesus Christ.[14] This is a source of great celebration! We praise "the exceeding great goodness of God, which would have nothing hid from us" and which shows us how to live in right ways, well, and blessedly."[15]

God gives the Scriptures to instruct us in salvation through Jesus Christ. "In the word of God, delivered to us by the prophets and apostles," wrote Bullinger, "is abundantly contained the whole effect of godliness, and what things soever are available to the leading of our lives rightly, well, and holily [blessedly]."[16] Bullinger cited 2 Timothy 3:16–17: "All scripture is inspired by God and is useful for teaching, for reproof, for correction, and for training in righteousness, so that everyone who belongs to God may be proficient, equipped for every good work." Bullinger believed Scripture provides "the confirmation of doctrines, and the rejection of all errors," and we are called on to follow Scripture this way. Scripture is a sure source of "doctrine" or teaching for "instruction in all duties of piety," as Bullinger put it in

13. Bullinger, *Decades*, 1:57.
14. See Bullinger, *Decades*, 1:60.
15. See Bullinger, *Decades*, 1:60.
16. Bullinger, *Decades*, 1:61.

the Second Helvetic Confession.[17] Scripture provides "the absolute doctrine of godliness."[18] All we need for salvation is found in Holy Scripture, "the Word of God." Scripture is sufficient for belief and behavior (cf. 1 Tim 3:14–15).

Scripture and Preaching

The Scriptures are made known to us as we read them and hear them proclaimed. Preaching is the means God uses to bring the message of salvation in Jesus Christ into the lives of women and men. Preaching is the means by which faith comes to life—by the power of the Holy Spirit.

Bullinger saw faith as the means by which we receive the benefits of what Jesus Christ has done in bringing salvation through his death on the cross (Rom 5:8). Faith is established within us by the work of the Holy Spirit (Eph 2:8–9). As Jesus said, "No one can come to me unless drawn by the Father who sent me" (John 6:44; cf. Matt 16:17). Said Bullinger: "Faith therefore is poured into our hearts by God, who is the well-spring and cause of all goodness."[19] Faith is the way we grasp God's promises to us in Jesus Christ. The love of God is poured into our hearts by the Holy Spirit who is given to us (Rom 5:5). We receive faith as God's gift; and the Holy Spirit given to us is God's gift. Our whole salvation is God's work!

How does faith come to us? Bullinger wrote that "God, in giving and inspiring faith, doth not use his absolute power, or miracles, in working; but a certain ordinary means agreeable to man's capacity: although he can indeed give faith without those means, to whom, when, and how it

17. Cochrane, ed., *Reformed Confessions*, 224.
18. Bullinger, *Decades*, 1:63. Cf. 61.
19. Bullinger, *Decades*, 1:84.

pleaseth him."[20] God could have by almighty power reached down and miraculously "zapped" people with faith! But instead, God uses "ordinary means" adjusted to human capacities. Faith comes by the work of the Holy Spirit in ways humans can receive. Christian faith becomes expressed in the church through its sacraments, baptism and the Lord's Supper.

God sends teachers and preachers to proclaim the message of Jesus Christ and the salvation humans can receive in him. God could send an angel from heaven to bestow faith in Christ. But God uses human beings to proclaim God's Word. Through that proclamation in preaching, faith is given. Bullinger wrote: "God himself alone, by sending his Holy Spirit into the hearts and minds of men, doth open our hearts, persuade our minds, and cause us with all our heart to believe that which we by his word and teaching have learned to believe."[21]

This led Bullinger to confess in the Second Helvetic Confession: "The Preaching of the Word of God Is the Word of God." He wrote:

> Wherefore when this Word of God is now preached in the church by preachers lawfully called, we believe that the very Word of God is proclaimed, and received by the faithful; and that neither any other Word of God is to be invented nor is to be expected from heaven: and that now the Word itself which is preached is to be regarded, not the minister that preaches; for even if he be evil and a sinner, nevertheless the Word of God remains still true and good.[22]

20. Bullinger, *Decades*, 1:84.
21. Bullinger, *Decades*, 1:85.
22. Cochrane, ed., *Reformed Confessions*, 225.

Preaching is the means God uses for God's Word to come to us so faith may be born in us by the Holy Spirit. While "God can illuminate whom and when he will, even without the external ministry, for that is in his power; but we speak of the usual way of instructing men, delivered unto us from God, both by commandment and example."[23]

Bullinger recognizes the Word of God is given to us as: the *incarnate* Word—Jesus Christ; the *written* Word—Holy Scripture; and the *proclaimed* Word—preaching. This shows the power of God's Word to reach us in ways we humans can receive.

SCRIPTURE AND THE CHURCH

Scripture is authoritative for us because it is God's Word. The Bible contains and teaches what we need to know and receive for salvation and living the life of faith so we can live in accord with God's will for us. Scripture is sufficient to convey everything we need for salvation. The church, Bullinger taught, has the responsibility—and opportunity—to preserve and witness to the Scriptures. The church is to publish the Scriptures in the sense of sharing them with the world. The church is to discern true Scripture from false scripture; and the church is to interpret Scripture. Those teachings of theologians and church traditions, including church councils, can be believed when they are in accord with biblical teachings. Other traditions, not grounded in Scripture, are to be rejected. Thus, the church rejects heresies, on the basis of Holy Scripture. Throughout all his writings, Bullinger emphasized these themes about the nature and authority of Scripture. In short: "We must all therefore beware, we must all watch, and stick fast unto the word of

---

23. Cochrane, ed., *Reformed Confessions*, 225.

God, which is left to us in the scriptures by the prophets and apostles."[24]

The Interpretation of Scripture

The Scriptures are God's Word. But the Scriptures need interpretation. The Bible is an ancient library of books written by people centuries before the sixteenth century when Bullinger lived. The Christian church has always recognized the need for biblical interpretation. Through the history of the church, many approaches to interpretation and ways of interpreting the Bible have been practiced. Well-meaning Christians have disagreed with each other over issues of biblical interpretation. These disagreements have frequently meant the creation of new church bodies. So biblical interpretations have consequences! This was especially so during the period of the sixteenth-century Protestant Reformation.

Interpreting Holy Scripture

Bullinger's preaching and teaching in Zurich was focused on interpreting the Bible. He sought to convey the message of Scripture, to listen to the Word of God, and to proclaim what is revealed in Holy Scripture. The public exercises of "prophesying" held regularly in the city had as their purpose the interpretation of Scripture. Ministers were to interpret the Bible under the guidance of the Holy Spirit. The conviction of Bullinger and his colleagues was that by using the methods of interpretation at hand, including humanist tools of language and textual criticism, the message of the Word of God could be clearly understood and thus proclaimed. A focus of this type of biblical interpretation

---

24. Bullinger, *Decades*, 1:69.

was on the practical Christian lives of Zurich's citizens. The goal was to make Scripture's message clear so everyone would know what it meant to follow Jesus Christ. To do this, in addition to listening to preaching, persons could be instructed on the meaning of biblical passages. In its subsequent editions, the Zurich Bible—first produced in the city in 1531—featured ways of trying to make Scripture more comprehensible: chapter outlines, marginal notes, and cross references. These helped guide readers of the text. Being educated on how to read Scripture was an ongoing task for Zurich Christians. Bullinger led in efforts to shape the Zurich Bible and its presentation of the biblical text.

Bullinger acknowledged some people believe the Scriptures as the "very word of God, is of itself so dark, that it cannot be read with any profit at all."[25] But often in Bullinger's biblical commentaries, he indicated the difficulties in biblical interpretation lay not with the biblical texts as much as with us—and our failures to use the resources God gives us for interpretation.

Others, said Bullinger, affirmed that "the word plainly delivered by God to mankind doth stand in need of no exposition: And therefore say they, that the scriptures ought indeed to be read of all men, but so that every man may lawfully invent and choose to himself such a sense as every one shall be persuaded in himself to be most convenient."[26] Or, in other words, anyone can read the Bible and choose any meaning that is "most convenient."

But Bullinger maintained the trust and

> hope that I have in God's goodness, that I am able plainly to declare, that to the godly the scripture is nothing dark at all, and that the Lord's will is altogether to have us understand

25. Bullinger, *Decades*, 1:70.
26. Bullinger, *Decades*, 1:70.

> it: then, that the scriptures ought always to be expounded. Where also I will teach you the manner, and some ready ways, how to interpret the scriptures. The handling of these points shall take away the impediments which drive men from the reading of the word of God, and shall cause the reading and hearing of the word of God to be both wholesome and fruitful.[27]

Bullinger's writings—biblical commentaries, sermons, and theological treatises—were based in biblical interpretation. One of his central convictions was always that "the truth and unity of the Church chiefly lies" not in its "outward rites and ceremonies" but in "the truth and unity of the catholic faith. This catholic faith is not given to us by human laws, but by Holy Scriptures, of which the Apostles' Creed is a compendium."[28] Creeds, for Bullinger, express the faith found in Scripture and are interpretations of Scripture.

In his Second Helvetic Confession, Bullinger succinctly listed key elements of biblical interpretation which he carried out as he spent his life and labors interpreting the Word of God. Before this list, Bullinger cited 2 Peter 1:20: "no prophecy of scripture is a matter of one's own interpretation." This means rejecting an "anything goes" approach, not allowing "all possible interpretations." Bullinger also rejected interpretations by the Roman Catholic Church, which he said wants to thrust its interpretations upon all for acceptance. Bullinger's conviction was that "the Church does not judge according to its own pleasure, but according to the sentence of the Holy Spirit and the order and rule of the Holy Scriptures."[29]

27. Bullinger, *Decades*, 1:70–71.
28. Cochrane, ed., *Reformed Confessions*, 267–68.
29. Bullinger, *Zwingli and Bullinger*, 323.

On biblical interpretation, Bullinger wrote:

> We hold that interpretation of the Scripture to be orthodox and genuine which is gleaned from the Scriptures themselves (from the nature of the language in which they were written, likewise according to the circumstances in which they were set down, and expounded in the light of like and unlike passages and of many and clearer passages) and which agree with the rule of faith and love, and contributes much to the glory of God and man's salvation.[30]

Bullinger's prescriptions for biblical interpretation were grounded in the conviction that Scripture interprets Scripture. Biblical passages or texts that are hard to understand should be interpreted in light of other biblical passages or texts that are more plain and easier to understand and interpret. "Scripture interprets Scripture" also means people should not jump to the writings of later theologians because they believe biblical passages are obscure or too difficult to understand.

Bullinger believed methods of biblical interpretation could include historical and rhetorical studies. He emphasized the importance of understanding biblical passages from their original languages—Hebrew for the Old Testament; Greek for the New Testament. Useful theological understandings can emerge only when they are based on sound interpretations of texts in their original languages.

Along with this were concerns to understand the contexts of biblical passages, what precedes and follows a passage, the words of the biblical texts and their meanings, and different ways words are used: tropes—figurative use of language; and sometimes allegories. A most important and reliable method for interpretation is the comparison of

30. Cochrane, ed., *Reformed Confessions*, 226.

Scripture passages with each other. To do this means one needs to be acquainted with the whole of Scripture and put in diligent practice and effort to interpret the Scriptures.

Also, Bullinger urged a concern for the "scope" (Lat. *scopus*) of Scripture. That is, to understand and recognize the purpose of Scripture. Most broadly, Scripture proclaims God and God's works; in the New Testament, the focus is on Christ and his works. So, Scripture should be interpreted in light of what Scripture intends to communicate, supremely: God's love for the world in Jesus Christ.

For Bullinger, a primary expression of God's purposes—found throughout the all the biblical books—is God's testament or covenant made with the human race (Genesis 17; 22). God's covenantal relationship with humans involve God's promises in covenants; and human obedience in keeping what God desires in the covenant. This means complete commitment and dedication to God and the strongest desire to do God's will. Covenants show the kind of God who is revealed in Scripture and ways the divine/human relationship with God's covenant people have been lived out through the whole of Scripture. For Bullinger, God's covenant is the same in the Old and the New Testaments.

Interpreting Scripture is not merely an intellectual exercise, according to Bullinger. This is captured in his prescription that our biblical interpretation should "agree with the rule of faith and love" (Second Helvetic Confession). St. Augustine and other theologians had spoken of this perspective as underlying all efforts to interpret Scripture. The Spirit who inspired Scripture is the best interpreter of Scripture. All human interpreters should approach the Bible with prayer and reverence. As Bullinger put it in his *Decades*:

> The most effectual rule of all, whereby to expound the word of God, is an heart that loveth

> God and his glory, not puffed up with pride, not desirous of vainglory, not corrupted with heresies and evil affections; but which doth continually pray to God for his holy Spirit, that, as by it the scripture was revealed and inspired, so also by the same Spirit it may be expounded to the glory of God and safeguard of the faithful.[31]

Bullinger went on to say that "the perfect exposition of God's word doth differ nothing from the rule of true faith and the love of God and our neighbour."[32]

Holy Scripture

For Heinrich Bullinger, the Word of God was Holy Scripture. In Scripture, God speaks. In the Bible, God's message is conveyed. In preaching, God's Word is heard through the human voice of the preacher. Scripture is foundational. Scripture is the Word of God. It is a sure and certain authority.

Scripture is inspired by the Holy Spirit. Its words are the words of its human authors. Bullinger does not present a theory of how the Scriptures were inspired. What was certain, he taught, is that in and through the Scripture God's voice is heard; and God's Word is revealed and given to the church.

Scripture is authoritative because it is God's revelation. Bullinger rejected the Roman Catholic view that Scripture gained its authority from the church and that church tradition held an equal role of authority for the church. Scripture carries its own evidence within itself that it is the Word of God.

Scripture is the sufficient source through which we learn of the salvation God brings to the world in Jesus Christ. In Scripture is presented all that is necessary for

---

31. Bullinger, *Decades*, 1:79.
32. Bullinger, *Decades*, 1:81. See Romans 12:3, 6.

salvation through faith in Jesus Christ, by the work of the Holy Spirit. Scripture is sufficient as the means through which people can come to faith in Christ and be guided in the ways God wants them to live as disciples of Jesus Christ. Scripture achieves its saving purpose.

Scripture is to be interpreted using human means and the processes. It is also to be interpreted under the guidance of the Holy Spirit. To accept Scripture as God's Word moves one into seeing all life from God's perspective and to live in this light.

Ultimately, for Bullinger: "We know very well that the Scripture is not called the Word of God because of the human voice, the ink and paper, or the printed letters (which all can be comprehended by the flesh), but because the meaning, which speaks through the human voice or is written with pen and ink on paper, is not originally from men, but is God's word, will, and meaning."[33]

QUESTIONS FOR DISCUSSION

1. What is the importance for Bullinger of maintaining that Scripture is the "Word of God" written by "human authors"?

2. What is the significance of Bullinger's view that Scripture is prior to the church since the "author" of Scripture is God?

3. What are ways the authority of Scripture shapes the lives of churches and the lives of Christians?

4. What resources for biblical interpretation did Bullinger use; and what are helpful resources for biblical interpretation today?

---

33. Dowey, *Commentary*, 204–5.

3

GOD

GOD IS THE SUBJECT of theology. Who is God? How do we know God? When we speak of God, what are we saying? Is it even proper for us to try to describe who God is and what he does? Isn't every human description of God essentially inaccurate? Can the mortal even grasp the immortal? All of these questions have haunted Christian theologians since the very first moment that people began to wonder about the Divine. Heinrich Bullinger too wrestled with the concept of God and the person of God, like Jacob wrestled with the angel at the brook. And, like Jacob, all who wrestle with God are hobbled by the encounter.

In this chapter we will investigate, with Bullinger as our guide, the person and work of God. Understanding, from the very outset, that we shall never, this side of eternity, know God fully. But we can know what God has revealed of himself, and in that light, Heinrich Bullinger has a great deal to show us.[1]

---

1. The details to follow are more fully developed, along with others, in Stephens' *Theology*, 93–124.

KNOWING GOD

Heinrich Bullinger preached a very large number of sermons. Many of those sermons were collected and published in a very expansive edition titled *The Decades*. That collection consists of fifty sermons divided into five large themes (Decades) of ten sermons each. The first Decade contains sermons on Scripture, faith, and the Apostles' Creed. The second Decade's topic is the law. The third Decade too is an exposition of the law (that is, as it is found in the Ten Commandments and ceremonial laws). The fourth Decade takes readers through topics like grace, repentance, and, relevant to our present discussion, God (Father, Son, and Spirit). And, finally, the fifth Decade concerns the church, prayer, sacraments, and practical issues like marriage and funerals, etc.

It is interesting that Bullinger does not broach the topic of God fully (though he naturally touches on it throughout) until the fourth Decade. First, he believes that we must fully grasp Scripture, the Creed, the Commandments, and the law before we are prepared sufficiently to approach the topic of the Lord Almighty. As he states it in the introduction to his sermons on God:

> I HAVE hitherto in thirty-two sermons discoursed upon the word of God, and the lawful exposition of the same; upon christian faith, the love of God and our neighbour. I have also spoken of the law of nature, of man's law, and God's law, and of the parts of God's law, namely, the moral, the ceremonial, and the judicial laws; of the use of the law, and of the fulfilling and abrogation of the same; of the likeness and difference betwixt the two testaments and people, the old and the new; of christian liberty; of offences; of the effect and merits of good works; of sin, and

> the sundry sorts thereof: and also of the grace of
> God, or the gospel of Jesu Christ, in whom our
> heavenly Father hath given us all things belonging to life and eternal salvation: finally, I have
> treated of repentance, and of the things that do
> especially seem to belong thereunto.[2]

Many theologians before, and after, Bullinger had approached any discussion of God from the starting point of philosophy. Bullinger too makes use of philosophical terminology, but only as strained through his own understanding, which was thoroughly scripturally based.

> Let no man therefore, that goeth about to know
> any certainty of God, descend into himself to
> search him out with thoughts of his own; neither
> let him ground his opinion upon men's determinations and weak definitions: for otherwise he
> shall always worship the invention of his own
> heart, mere folly, trifles and foolish phantasies.[3]

For Bullinger, Scripture is the starting point of our understanding of God. Philosophers, in the famous phrase of Tertullian, "Are the patriarchs of heretics". If we wish to know God, we must start where God reveals himself, and for Bullinger, that is Scripture and Scripture alone. Hence Bullinger's procedure of preaching on Scripture before he preaches on the person of God.

Before we can properly apprehend God (inasmuch as we can apprehend God at all) we must disabuse ourselves of the falsehoods we hold in our understanding of God. Bullinger notes:

> Concerning God there were of old many erroneous opinions, not among the ruder sort of

2. Bullinger, *Decades*, 4:123.
3. Bullinger, *Decades*, 4:125.

God

people only, but even in the whole pack of philosophers, and conventicles of false Christians.[4]

To have a proper view of God, Bullinger asserts, one must have faith. Lacking faith means lacking the necessary attribute for the proper understanding of God's self disclosure in Scripture. Those without faith simply cannot understand who God is. And that is why there are so many false and inaccurate notions of God in the world. Bullinger remarks, "God can rightly be known only from the word of God and that he is to be believed and received as he reveals himself to us in his word."

Bullinger also makes it quite clear that our knowledge of God is something that has limits. And those who wish to go beyond the limits that God has set to our knowledge of him are treading in very dangerous territory. Drawing from the Old Testament example of those who exceeded the boundaries of propriety, Bullinger notes:

> He of old among the Israelites was stricken through and slain, which passed beyond the bounds that the Lord had limited out: and we also have certain appointed bounds about the knowledge of God, which to pass is hurtful unto us; yea, it is punished with assured death.[5]

That warning is intended to offer Christians the opportunity to exercise all due humility. And yet, with those boundaries well in mind, Christians are expected to both know God and to love and serve God. And for that, they must possess faith.

To be sure, people can know that there *is* a God even if they have no faith. But they will never know *God* until faith

---

4. Bullinger, *Decades*, 4:124.
5. Bullinger, *Decades*, 4:173.

is activated in their lives. Knowing God means having faith in God. Having faith in God means knowing God.

God, however, knows the weakness and frailty of humanity and accordingly he accommodates himself, in Scripture, to that frailty and weakness. He teaches us, in Scripture, just what we are capable of understanding. Nothing more and nothing less. To try to understand more than Scripture reveals about God will lead to dangerous and heretical speculation. To try to understand less than Scripture teaches is to fall victim to an inadequate understanding of the person and work of God. Scripture, then, in Bullinger's mind, strikes exactly the right balance and does so because it is God's self revelation to his people.

So, Bullinger advises, there are specific ways by which God can be known: 1) through the names of God, 2) through the visions and images contained in Scripture, 3) and most importantly, through Christ. But God can also be known through 4) his works. Furthermore, we can learn things about God through 5) the comparisons between God and others which we find in Scripture. Finally, we can know things about God 6) through the sayings of the prophets and apostles.

God, in Bullinger's theology, genuinely wishes to be known. So he reveals himself. And people of faith are those "insiders" who understand that revelation. People of faith can know God in his fullness, in his trinitarian manifestation. Which leads us to turn to a consideration of Bullinger's exposition of the doctrine of the Trinity.

THE TRINITY

It is no overstatement to say that the doctrine of the Trinity has baffled and stumped Christians since it first appeared on the theological horizon. Everyone, it seems, has an opinion about it. Some hold to it as to a life vest on the sea in a hurricane and others, like the Unitarians, have abandoned it altogether. Yet it is fair to say that orthodox Christians have accepted the doctrine since the beginning. Bullinger was one of them. And he was willing to fight for the doctrine, as his letter to Myconius on July 23, 1537 makes clear. In that letter he describes the views of certain anti-trinitarian radicals and assures Myconius that he will maintain the truth of the doctrine against them. And naturally, in his sermons, he asserts the same, writing "the true knowledge of God is that which recognizes that he is one in being and three in persons." His scriptural proofs for that claim also support, he insists, the conclusion that those texts "sufficiently prove that God is in substance one, and in being immense, eternal, spiritual." And though the word "Trinity" does not appear in Scripture, which alone is the ground of Bullinger's theology, the concept of the Trinity certainly does.

Bullinger writes (in his typically verbose style):

> True faith is in God the Father, and in the Son, not simply, but incarnate, and in the Holy Ghost. For the holy and consubstantial Trinity is distinguished by the differences of names, that is, by the properties of the persons. For the Father is the Father, and not the Son: and the Son is the Son, and not the Father: and the Holy Ghost is the Holy Spirit proper to the Father and the Son. For the substance of the Deity is all one, or the same: wherefore we preach not three, but one God. Therefore we must believe in God; but, distinctly and more fully expounding our faith, we must so believe, that we may refer the same glorification to every person. For there is no difference of faith. For we ought not to have a greater faith in the Father than in the Son, and in the Holy Ghost; but the measure and manner

> of it must be one and the same, equally consisting in each of the three persons: so that by this means we may confess the unity of nature in the trinity of persons.[6]

Bullinger's trinitarian theology is evident not only in the sermons, but in early works addressing important theological issues. Namely, in *The Two Natures of Christ* (1534) and *The Authority of Scripture* (1538). In those works he shows his willingness to accept scriptural "ideas" even when the very words used to describe those ideas are not present in the Bible. However, he also shows quite clearly that where an idea or concept cannot be grounded upon a scriptural foundation, it should be avoided.

The mystery of the Trinity cannot, however, be rationally explained. Instead of seeking infallible proofs for the doctrine, people of faith need simply to "steadfastly believe the clear word of God" on the subject. Christian teaching is, for Bullinger, practical and aimed at behavior and worship. The Trinity too is a doctrine whose aim is to shape behavior and worship. Bullinger observes "Therefore, when we read that God created the world, we understand that the Father from whom are all things, by the Son by whom are all things, in the Holy Spirit in whom are all things, created the world." This is the God we worship and serve.

GOD THE CREATOR

Bullinger was absolutely convinced, as were all the Reformation theologians, that God created the world in six literal days. In the sixteenth century there was no "big bang theory" or "theory of evolution" or "scientific view of the coming into being of the world." Bullinger was, however,

---

6. Bullinger, *Decades*, 4:168.

more concerned, as theology has always been, in the "why" of creation rather than the "how" of creation.

Bullinger was of the view that not only was the world literally created by God in six days; but that the creation itself is a demonstration of the power and might of God. Furthermore, the creation of all things was not something that God did merely as a lark. God made what he made, in the view of Bullinger, for mankind. God has made all things for us and has subjected all things to us. Why? Because he wishes us well, and he has the power to make it so.

But there's something more to the fact that God is the creator of all things and that is that God is also the sustainer of all things. God did not, in the view of Bullinger, simply set the world in motion and walk away from it (as the deists would believe centuries later). Instead, God created, and sustains, and he sustains by means of his providential care. In short, then, for Bullinger, creation and providence are two sides of the same coin. It is essential, then, that Bullinger's view of providence be considered in any discussion of his understanding of creation.

Bullinger's doctrine of providence centers on the belief that God not only sustains all things but preserves, rules, and provides for all things. Providence isn't the exercise of tyranny or the imposition of a tyrant's will; rather it is the loving provision of the Heavenly Father. Any understanding of Bullinger that suggests that his notion of providence is in line with fatalism or hyper-Calvinism is simply wrong from the start. God's will is good. And he acts on behalf of creation from the basis of that good will.

The scriptural foundation of Bullinger's doctrine of providence is "My Father works until now, and I work" (John 5:17); "God created the world through his Son and rules and upholds all things by his word of power" (Heb 1:2–3); "By God we live and move and are" (Acts 17:28);

and "God fills our hearts with food and gladness" (Acts 14:17).[7] In his own words, "By his providence he cares for the affairs of mortals and for all things created for the sake of man."[8]

Providence, furthermore, does not mean to Bullinger that God forces his will upon people. His scriptural proof for this is, among other texts, the fact that in the story of Lot at Sodom and Gomorrah, Lot is free to leave or stay, according to his own wishes. Providence is provision, not coercion.

Bullinger also sees a connection between freedom and providence in the fact that people both suffer the consequences of their sins and that even sinful people experience blessings from God. God, because of his love, wishes people well, even the sinful. In short, Bullinger writes, "The most wise and excellent governing of all things by his divine providence which is always just and most righteous" is a manifestation of "God's goodwill towards us," even when we clearly do not deserve that goodwill.[9]

GOD AS THE OBJECT OF WORSHIP

Bullinger's understanding of God, as sustainer and creator results in his understanding of God as the worthy object of worship. He remarks, opining that human beings are "not created or born to contemplate the stars . . . but to be the image and temple of God, in whom God might dwell and reign . . . [so that we] should therefore acknowledge God, revere, adore, invoke, and worship him, and so be joined to God and live with him eternally." People, in sum, are born to be in fellowship with God through worship. Any life that

---

7. Bullinger, *Decades*, 3:178.
8. Bullinger, *Decades*, 3:178–81.
9 Bullinger, *Decades*, 3:192–94.

fails to apprehend that simple fact is a life that is, essentially, wasted and meaningless. Our meaning as human beings is drawn precisely from our relationship with God.

This relationship with God, then, ought not be watered down by the worship of saints or images or creatures or anything else. God deserves, as sustainer and creator, our undivided attention. Worship of the saints only makes that impossible—hence its inherent sinfulness. Bullinger is also quite keen, in his discussion of the worship of the one true God, to insist that worship directed towards God is the only legitimate Christian variety of worship and worship directed towards saints, or anything else, is simply idolatry.

Furthermore, for Bullinger, merely going through the motions of worship (externally, bodily) is as insufficient as directing worship to the saints. The heart must be involved and engaged in the worship of God just as much as the body is engaged in being present at the church. As Bullinger observes, "outward worship immediately follows a mind rightly imbued with true faith and the holy fear of God." The body mirrors the heart and mind, in other words. Or should. And will, when worship is authentically happening. True worship is, then, a twofold act: internal and external. And the internal expresses itself externally. The work of the Spirit in the heart is manifested in the deeds of the hands. Scripture itself insists on this duality when it declares that true religion is to minister to the fatherless and the widow (Jas 1:27).

Bullinger also expresses the view that there are those who appear externally to be worshippers of God but in their hearts are far from God. They serve God on their terms, not on his. Bullinger views this as inadequate and forthrightly recommends repentance on their behalf lest they be absent from the Christian's everlasting heritage.

When it comes to prayer, as an act of worship and as an aspect of worship, Bullinger is quite clear, stating that for prayer to be effective and meaningful it requires "a faithful mind which acknowledges God to be the author and only giver of all good things, who wills to hear all who invoke him and who can grant all our requests and desires." Prayer, as is true of worship and every other aspect of the Christian life, requires faith. It was never more true for any theologian that "without faith, it is impossible to please God" (Heb 11:6).

> And of prayer chiefly there are two parts; invocation or asking, and thanksgiving. By petition we lay open unto God the requests and desires of our heart; beseeching him to give us good things, and that he will turn from us evil things, as may be to his glory and good pleasure, and according to our necessity. In invocation or petition we comprehend obsecration, which is a more vehement prayer; and also intercession, whereby we commend other men's matters to the Lord.[10]

***

The subject of Bullinger's theological work is God, as Father, Son, and Holy Spirit, made known through Scripture, the creator and sustainer of all things and the redeemer of humanity. God is the center of his theology.

In the chapters that follow, the work of God as made known through the works of the Son and the Holy Spirit will be examined in turn. But there is no doubt that for Bullinger, speaking of God means nothing less than speaking of the Father, the Son, and the Spirit. Bullinger cannot be rightly or justifiably accused of being "christocentric" theologically. Nor can he be understood to focus primarily

10. Bullinger, *Decades*, 5:163–64.

on the Spirit. Bullinger is *theo*logically focused: focused on the absolute centrality of the fullness of *God*, as God is in himself and as he manifests himself through the Son and the Spirit.

QUESTIONS FOR DISCUSSION

1. How is Bullinger's doctrine of God similar to your beliefs about God?
2. What do you find in Bullinger's theology of God that is most dissimilar to your own?
3. If you were to describe God, how do you think you would do it?

4

CHRIST

Jesus the Christ, the Savior of the world, the second member of the Trinity, is also, unsurprisingly, a central concern of Bullinger's theological enquiries.[1] To be sure, Bullinger's treatment of Christ in his sermons and in his theological treatises never comes first. Bullinger, as we have seen previously, always starts with Scripture and then turns to God the Father and God in his trinitarian form before he moves on to a discussion of the Son.

Bullinger doesn't do this because Christ is of secondary importance but rather because he is simply following historical precedent. The church for many centuries had followed the same theological path. That is, it set the stage for any discussion of God by describing how it is that God can be known. Only when that foundation is established can we speak with any confidence about God. Then, preachers and teachers very much should turn to a consideration of Christ. As he writes in the First Helvetic Confession, "... in

1. Cf. Stephens, *Theology*, 125–40.

all evangelical teaching the most sublime and the principal article and the one that should be expressly set forth in every sermon and impressed upon people's hearts should be that we are preserved and saved solely by the one mercy of God and by the merit of Christ."

CHRIST AS THE CENTER OF SCRIPTURE

Who, then, is Christ? As all of the Reformers believed, rightly or wrongly, Christ was the center of not only the New Testament, but the Old as well. Christ, they perceived, was to be seen on every page and in every story, somehow or other, in the pages of the Old Testament. He was to be found in the story of the Garden of Eden as the one who would "crush the serpent's head" and he was found in the prophetic texts like Isaiah 7:14 and he was even discernible in such erotic texts as the Song of Solomon, where his love for the church is proclaimed through the vivid imagery of an ancient Hebrew poem about love. In short, in a famous phrase of Luther, every page is the cradle in which Christ lies.

This anachronistic reading of the Hebrew Bible was simply the way it was read during the sixteenth century and it was simply the way it was read by Bullinger himself. Taking that into account and recognizing it is a key to understanding Bullinger's beliefs about Christ, his office, and his ministry.

But when we turn to Bullinger's understanding of Christ as revealed in the New Testament we find significant differences between him and his contemporaries. Famously, for example, Luther disdained the Book of Revelation. Bullinger, however, did not. Rather, seeing its christological message quite clearly, he esteemed the book. In his series of sermons on it he wrote that the book is "most evangelical and apostolic." So where Luther found Christ primarily in Paul, Bullinger found Christ in the corners of the New Testament, and proclaimed him from those corners.

The basis of Bullinger's Christology, then, being every recess of both the Old and New Testaments, his Christology is quite full and multilayered. That fullness and richness of texture give Bullinger's doctrine of Christ a thoroughness that few other Reformation theologians achieve.

THE TWO NATURES OF CHRIST

Bullinger's earliest and fullest treatment of Christology as a separate theological investigation was written in 1534 and titled "The Two Natures of Christ." What are the two natures of Christ? They are his human and divine natures, for Jesus is both fully human and fully God. As such, he is the only agent of our redemption.

From very early days the church debated the divinity and the humanity of Christ. On one extreme there were people who taught that Jesus was simply a human being like any other human being. The theologians of the early church found this view wanting. Yes, Jesus Christ was a fully human person. In this way, he identified with sinful humanity and in his death, he died "for" sinful humanity. But more is needed. For Jesus' death to be meaningful and to bring salvation Jesus must be more than a human alone. A human death cannot save us—*only God* can save us. Only God has the power to defeat sin and death. Jesus was fully human and fully divine. By being divine, his death has the power to save sinful humans; and to bring the forgiveness of sins that all humans need. The church maintained both Jesus' full humanity and his full divinity because both are necessary if human sinners are to receive salvation through the death of Jesus Christ on the cross.

Christ

On the other extreme were those who insisted that Jesus was fully divine and that there were no aspects of humanity in him. This too caused the early church's theologians to be uncomfortable. They reasoned that God, being incapable of dying, could not possibly die for the sins of humanity. He could "appear" to die, but he could not really die. And "appearing" to die is not the same thing as actually dying and serving as an authentic sacrifice for sin.

The solution the church reached, and which Bullinger adopted, as did all of the Reformation theologians, is that Christ was both fully human and fully divine. Like the doctrine of the Trinity, this solution did not solve the problem but it did remove it to the realm of "mystery" and that was sufficient for the church. There are things we simply cannot comprehend. The fact that Jesus was both fully human *and* fully divine is one of those mysteries.

But Bullinger is not at all interested in maintaining the doctrine in order to speculate about how Christ can be both fully human and fully divine. Instead, his singular concern is that we know who Christ is as fully divine and fully human so that we find comfort in the fact that as such he is our redeemer. Simply stated, he strives to show "what great love of the Father toward us is revealed to us in Christ" in salvation. This act of bringing salvation to God's wandering children is, in fact, the single purpose of being the savior of the world. In Bullinger's own words, "the Son of God . . . was predestined or foreordained from eternity . . . to be the savior of the world."

CHRIST IN THE APOSTLES' CREED

Heinrich Bullinger found the Creed to be a rich resource for Christian theology. His remarks on its contents can be seen as his commentary on that ancient text. Accordingly, on the second article of the Creed, on Jesus the Christ, Bullinger comments:

> For the second article of the christian faith is thus word for word: "And in Jesus Christ, his only Son, our Lord." This article also comprehendeth two things: the first is, that we believe in the Son of God; the second, what the Son of God is. For we confess that we believe, that is, that we put our whole hope and confidence of life and salvation, as well in the Son as in the Father. And therefore we say plainly, "I believe in Jesus Christ," even as before we said, "I believe in God," &c.[2]

The two things that the Creed teaches about Jesus are, first, that Jesus is the Son of God. This profoundly rich theological concept will be fully fleshed out in Bullinger's other sermons and works. In sum, the Son of God is our redeemer and as redeemer, he is also our Lord and king as well as high priest. And the second aspect of the Creed's declaration, Bullinger believes, is that being the Son of God has important implications. These aspects of Jesus' redemptive act are inseparable and virtually indistinguishable. Yet, like a diamond held up to the light whose many facets glisten with different shades of color, so too the fullness of who Jesus is and what he achieved is made more beautiful when held up to view and its different aspects seen.

Important, too, to Bullinger is the fact that the Christ is a particular, single, known person: Jesus. This needs to be pointed out, Bullinger asserts, because

> the second thing that is to be marked is, that the name of the only-begotten Son of God is opened, and he is called "Jesus Christ." The name is expressly set down, that we may know

2. Bullinger, *Decades*, 4:127.

Christ

who it is in whom we believe, lest peradventure we might be deceived in the person.[3]

Our redeemer is not Judas nor John the Baptist nor Isaiah nor any other person in history. Do not be deceived, Bullinger advises. There is no other redeemer. There is no other Christ but the one, Jesus.

Finally, the third point Bullinger wishes to make about the Second Article of the Creed, is that

> The last thing that is to be noted now in this second article is, that we call the Son of God "our Lord." The Son of God verily is for two causes properly called our Lord: first, in respect of the mystery of our redemption . . . .[4]

The Lordship of Christ is perhaps one of the most important aspects of his deity for Bullinger. Jesus is Lord. It was the earliest church's earliest confession. Its implications are gigantic. The Lordship of Christ is the cornerstone of Christian ethics and behavior. As Lord, he is "commander" and "master" and is owed our highest and single loyalty. He, as Lord, has the right to direct our paths and any variation from his direction is a denial and abandonment of his lordship. Quite pointedly, Bullinger states:

> Christ is the Lord of all the elect, whom he hath delivered from the power and dominion of Satan, sin, and death, and hath made them a people of his own getting for himself.[5]

Christ's lordship means a transfer of ownership and dominion. The elect (a concept to which we will return later in this volume) belong to Satan no longer; nor do they

3. Bullinger, *Decades*, 4:128.

4. Bullinger, *Decades*, 4:129.

5. Bullinger, *Decades*, 4:129.

belong to sin or death either. They are Christ's own and are obliged to behave as such.

CHRIST IN BULLINGER'S SERMONS

How all this works out in Bullinger's preaching is made apparent in his sermons on Christ in the *Decades*. In particular, sermons thirty-six and thirty-seven are the most fertile ground for harvesting Bullinger's Christology. Thirty-six focuses on the more refined theological aspects of Christology like Christ's consubstantiality with the Father. Thirty-seven turns to a broader consideration of the threefold office of Christ.

Bullinger states his thesis clearly at the beginning of sermon thirty-seven:

> Christ Jesus is a king; therefore he is Lord of all, ruler and governor of all things which are in heaven and in earth, and specially of the catholic church itself, which is the communion of saints. And for so much as he is King and Lord, truly by his royal or kingly office he is the deliverer or preserver, the revenger and defender, and, finally, the lawgiver of his elect.[6]

Christ is king. Bullinger will go on to also describe Christ as priest. The office of Christ, then, as "priest, and king," is a core aspect of Bullinger's teaching on Jesus the Christ.

JESUS IS KING

That Christ is king is no mere slogan for Bullinger. The fact that Christ is king is important because kings rule and Christ as king is our ruler, our sovereign, our master. All of

6. Bullinger, *Decades*, 4:273.

this is very real to Bullinger and he insists on the implications of the fact. Jesus must be both followed and obeyed. As king, he rules our lives absolutely. As king, he has ultimate authority. As king, he is owed fealty. As king, he is owed our very lives. But most especially, the kingdom of this king is the church. "Therefore the church, the communion or fellowship of saints, being obedient and subject to their king Christ, is called the kingdom of God."[7] This notion and the others are not new to our understanding of Bullinger, as he has already made these points before, most notably in the sermon on the Apostles' Creed. But Bullinger is not of the mind that people can be told something only once and grasp it. Rather, the truth must be constantly reiterated and reinforced.

Bullinger makes it very clear that this kingdom of God is a spiritual kingdom and that those who live in it are subjects of the king, Christ. We will discuss the church more fully later on. For now, our point is simply that the king of the church is Christ and that his reign over the people of God is everlasting.

Jesus is also priest. To this issue we now turn.

JESUS AS PRIEST

That Bullinger believed Jesus to be found in the Old Testament has already been described. It is, then, not at all surprising that Jesus is also found not just broadly in the Old Testament but specifically as well in particular persons and events. Chiefly, for Bullinger, Jesus is found prefigured in the priesthood. He remarks "And now Christ our Lord is a priest, yea, that chiefest, only, and everlasting priest, whom the high priests of the old people did prefigure and shadow

7. Bullinger, *Decades*, 4:275.

out."[8] He then proceeds to show how this is made clear in the Book of Hebrews.

More substantially, Bullinger thinks that

> when we read that the office of priests in times past was to serve in the tabernacle, to teach the people, to make intercession between God and men, to pray for the people and to bless them, to sacrifice also, and to consecrate or sanctify; and that now it is manifest that Jesus Christ is the lawful priest; it is certain that he is tied to the selfsame offices, but indeed to so much more excellent than these by how much he hath obtained a more excellent priesthood.[9]

The reason that the priesthood of Jesus is so important to Bullinger and the other Reformers is because they are certain that Jesus' death was a substitutionary sacrifice in which and through which the eternal Son of God died in the place of evil and sinful humanity and bore the penalty of their sins in his body on the cross. This substitution of Jesus Christ in the place of sinners as a view of the atonement was a central way the church understood the meaning of Christ's death on the cross as atonement for human sin. Jesus "took our place" and "died for our sins" were main ways the church had confessed its faith in the atonement for centuries, before Bullinger arrived on the scene. No one questioned it with any seriousness. That being the case, Jesus' portrayal as high priest who administers the sacrifice and Lamb of God who is slain for the sins of the world was both intriguing and extraordinary. For the Old Testament never associates the office of the high priest with the sacrificial victim. The high priest doesn't become the sacrifice, he offers it. And the Lamb doesn't offer itself, it is offered.

8. Bullinger, *Decades*, 4:282.

9. Bullinger, *Decades*, 4:283.

Christ

Combining the one who offers the sacrifice and the sacrificial victim into one character is unique to Christian theology, and Bullinger feels no compulsion to explain away the apparent logical inconsistency of such a view nor the fact that the Old Testament never provides material for such a leap.

Bullinger does not, however, simply describe the sacrifice of Jesus as the only aspect of his priesthood. He also focuses attention on Jesus the intercessor. Jesus prays. And he prays for his people. He makes this obvious when he writes:

> Christ our high priest maketh intercession for all the saints in his own temple. For he, being the only advocate and patron of all the faithful, prayeth to the Father for us on the right hand of God; for he ascended unto the right hand of God the Father, that he should always appear there in the presence of God, to follow all our suits faithfully: of which thing I have spoken more at large in my last sermon, where I entreated of invocation and intercession. The same our Lord only blesseth us.[10]

Jesus, the Lord and high priest; these themes are central in Bullinger's preaching about him. But there's something else that is intriguing about Bullinger's treatment of Jesus, and that is that here, while speaking of Christ, Bullinger decides to speak more fully about the duties of the Christian person.

JESUS AND THE CHRISTIAN LIFE

In the midst of his sermon on Jesus, Bullinger remarks "Here this place requireth to speak somewhat of the name

10. Bullinger, *Decades*, 4:284.

of a Christian, and of the duties of a christian man."[11] Then follows in the sermon a discussion of the importance of living out the full meaning of the fact that we bear the name of Christ and are called after him; Christians. To be sure, Christ is not his surname (as people sometimes seem to believe) so it is not merely his surname that we bear, but his very image. As he puts it rather plainly, "We see what the duty of Christians is; namely, to maintain this dignity even to the last gasp, lest it be taken from us again by Satan."[12] That means that we who bear his name should act as he acts and do as he does and pray as he prays and speak as he speaks and reflect him in every aspect of life. When people see Christians, they are meant to see Christ.

The benefit of such a lifestyle and commitment is that the followers of Jesus overcome the world through their faith. But that is not the end of the matter. Bullinger extrapolates from the image of Christ, who is priest and king, that his disciples are also kings and priests. He stresses the "kingship" of Christians in connection with their overcoming the prince of this world, Satan. And he stresses the priestly aspect of the Christian life and its manifold responsibilities. He notes:

> Again, because we are Christians, that is to say, anointed, surely we are priests also; and therefore, according to our priestly office, we teach, we admonish, we exhort, and comfort all our brethren, and all men that are committed to our charge. Where notwithstanding we do necessarily make a difference between the christian priesthood and the ecclesiastical ministry. All Christians truly, as well men as women, are priests, but we are not all ministers

11. Bullinger, *Decades*, 4:289.
12. Bullinger, *Decades*, 4:289.

> of the church: for we cannot all one with another preach publicly, administer the sacraments, and execute other duties of pastors, unless we be lawfully called and ordained thereunto.[13]

So while Bullinger fully accepts the "priesthood of all believers" he also makes sure to maintain the distinctions between the clergy and the laity. This distinction is not merely formal or symbolic but extraordinarily important. This distinction is made even clearer in Bullinger's treatment of the church, to which we will shortly turn.

When he turns to an evaluation of how Christians are doing, on the whole, being the people of God who reign as kings and who act as priests, he finds his contemporaries wanting. Bullinger was of the opinion that Christians should act like Christ. He writes:

> if we behold ourselves in this looking-glass of a christian name, we shall see that very few at this day are worthy of this name. Truly all of us are commonly so called, and we will be named Christians; but few of us live a life worthy of our profession.[14]

One wonders what Bullinger would think of today's Christians of America. What he thought of his compatriots on the matter engendered some of his sharpest criticism and though Bullinger was a peacemaker at heart—who never sought out conflict of any sort, though he did not fear it when it arrived on his doorstep—at this point he let fly his unhappiness. Especially at the Roman Catholics who, he opined, were more concerned with worshiping the pope than they were with worshiping Christ.

---

13. Bullinger, *Decades*, 4:290.
14. Bullinger, *Decades*, 4:293.

Our evaluation of Bullinger's doctrine of Christ will conclude the same way he concludes his sermon on Christ:

> with these words of St Augustine: "The Son of God, which made us, is made among us; and being our king ruleth us: and therefore we are Christians, because he is Christ. He is called Christ a Chrismate, that is to say, of anointing. Kings also and priests were anointed, and he was anointed king and priest. Being a king, he fought for us: being a priest, he offered himself for us. When he fought for us, he was as it were overcome, yet by right he hath overcome in very deed: for he was crucified, and on his cross whereon he was nailed he slew the devil, and then he was our king . . . ." To Him be glory for ever and ever. Amen.[15]

Amen.

QUESTIONS FOR DISCUSSION

1. In Bullinger's theology, how important is Jesus for the salvation of believers?

2. What are the benefits of knowing Christ, for Bullinger?

3. Is the doctrine of Christ a subset of the doctrine of God, or is it a separate doctrine for Bullinger?

4. Why do you think Christology matters to Bullinger?

---

15. Bullinger, *Decades*, 4:296.

5

HOLY SPIRIT

THE HOLY SPIRIT IS an important part of Heinrich Bullinger's thought. The Spirit impacts Bullinger's theology of the Trinity, Holy Scripture, salvation, Word, and sacraments. Bullinger's attention to the Holy Spirit appears throughout his writings. But he did not devote a separate chapter to the Spirit in his Second Helvetic Confession. In one sense, Bullinger's treatment of the Spirit is similar to the Spirit's work in the New Testament. There, the Spirit does not draw attention to the Spirit but rather points to or witnesses to Jesus Christ. Theologically, for Bullinger, the Spirit's work is to point to Christ, to be active in the church and in the lives of believers, but not to do so with great fanfare or attention to the Spirit. The Spirit witnesses to Jesus Christ as the center of the Christian gospel.

THE HOLY SPIRIT AND THE TRINITY

Basic to Christian belief is that God is one God in three persons: Father, Son, and Holy Spirit.[1] Each member of the Godhead is fully God. Bullinger is completely in line with orthodox Christian teaching. So, he can appeal to Scripture and to the writings of early church theologians and church councils in describing the Holy Spirit since the theologians and councils are expressing what the Scriptures also teach.

To begin with, Bullinger wrote that "the fathers taught, that the Father, the Son, and the Holy Ghost are one God. God in the most reverend Trinity, the maker and governor of heaven and earth and all things which are therein; by whom man was made, and who for man did make all things, and put all things under mankind, to minister unto him things necessary, as a loving Father and most bountiful Lord."[2] God is the "maker and governor of all things"—the creator of all. This God the creator is a triune God—a Trinity of persons. This God is a loving God, who loves humanity as a parent and as a Lord who wants to give to the creation and the humans who owe their existence to God.

Bullinger declared: "The Holy Ghost is the third person in Trinity to be worshipped, very God, proceeding from the Father and the Son, which enlighteneth, regenerateth, sanctifieth, and fulfilleth the faithful with all good graces." This is a "theological mouthful"! Bullinger's basics are:

1) The Spirit is fully a person of the Trinity and is equally worshiped as God, as are the Father and the Son. Bullinger cites biblical passages such as Matthew 28:19–20, John 14:26, 15:26, and 16:13–15 to substantiate this view. In a sermon on the Holy Spirit, Bullinger appealed to the

---

1. Cf. Bullinger, *Decades*, 4:156–58. Said Bullinger: "The Father is God, the Son is God, and the Holy Ghost is God, into whose name we are baptized," 4:161.

2. Bullinger, *Decades*, 1:43.

Holy Spirit

"Great Commission" of Jesus to his disciples: "Go therefore and make disciples of all nations, baptizing them in the name of the Father and of the Son and of the Holy Spirit" (Matt 28:19) and wrote that "surely this only sentence of our Saviour . . . doth abundantly confirm to godly minds that the Holy Ghost is the third person in Trinity."[3] The persons of the Trinity may be distinguished from each other; but cannot be divided from each other. The church believes: "According to the nature or essence they are so joined together that they are one God, and the divine nature is common to the Father, Son and Holy Spirit."[4]

2) The Spirit "proceeds from the Father and the Son." This was a debated theological question in the early church. In what became the Eastern (Greek) church, the view was that the Spirit proceeded only from the Father. In the Western (Latin) church, the orthodox theological view was that the Holy Spirit is the Spirit of both the Father and the Son and "proceeds" from both. This has been called the "double procession" of the Spirit. Biblical passages from John's Gospel (John 14–16; as well as Gal 4:6; and Matt 10:20) are used by Bullinger to substantiate this interpretation. In his sermons on the Book of Revelation (*Sermons on the Apocalypse*), Bullinger supported his view of the double procession by appealing to Revelation 4:5, since the Spirit is there shown as proceeding from the "throne" where "he that sits on the throne" (God) is there; but also the Lamb (Jesus Christ). Then, Bullinger put it succinctly: "To be short, if there is one substance and nature of the father and of the son, I see not how the holy ghost should proceed from the father, that he should not proceed of the son also. Let us

---

3. Bullinger, *Decades*, 4:300.

4. Cochrane, ed., *Reformed Confessions*, 228.

rather leave those scrupulous disputations to idle wits: let us believe, that the spirit proceedeth from both."[5]

3) The person of the Holy Spirit is important in light of what the New Testament sees as the work of the Holy Spirit. Bullinger speaks of this as the works of enlightening, regenerating, sanctifying, and fulfilling the faithful with all good graces. These are seen in relation to the Spirit and Holy Scripture, salvation, the Word, and sacraments.

THE HOLY SPIRIT AND SCRIPTURE

For Bullinger and other Protestant Reformers, Scripture gained its authority because it was inspired by the Holy Spirit. In his sermon on the Holy Ghost in his *Decades*, Bullinger said, "The prophets were believed to have prophesied by the inspiration of the Holy Spirit."[6] He also said "the Holy Ghost, which was wholly in the mind of Moses, directed his hand as he writ."[7] Bullinger did not develop a theory of biblical inspiration, to say "how" the Bible was inspired. What can be seen as clear from his statement here, however, is that God is the source of Moses' "inspiration." What God wanted written by Moses; was written by Moses. The foundation of Scripture's authority is that it is from God—"inspired" by God the Holy Spirit.

The Holy Spirit is also the interpreter of Scripture. In his Second Helvetic Confession, Bullinger cited 2 Peter 1:20, "No prophecy of scripture is a matter of one's own interpretation," to say that "the Holy Scriptures are not of

---

5. Cf. Bullinger, *Decades*, 4:306–10, and especially "for the Father is the Father, and not the Son: and the Son is the Son, and not the Father: and the Holy Ghost is the Holy Spirit proper to the Father and the Son," *Decades* 4:168.

6. Bullinger, *Decades*, 4:5. Cf. 4:119 and ch. 2 above.

7. Bullinger, *Decades*, 1:46.

private interpretation" and therefore, said Bullinger, "we do not allow all possible interpretations."[8] It is the Spirit who guides readers of Scripture into God's truth (cf. John 16:13). Thus the work of the Holy Spirit continues after the initial inspiration of the biblical text to the ongoing interpretation of the Scriptures by readers of Scripture in the present day. Scripture and Spirit are in relation to each other. Those who read Scripture should seek the guidance of the Holy Spirit, asking the Spirit to lead them in their reading and interpretation of it.

An important interpretive principle for Bullinger is that the Scriptures present and point us toward Jesus Christ. The Old Testament anticipates the coming of God's Messiah, Jesus Christ. The New Testament proclaims Jesus Christ as the Messiah and the savior of the world (John 3:16), who fulfills Old Testament prophecies. As we read Scripture under the guidance of the Holy Spirit, we will be led to see, as Bullinger wrote, that "Christ is the goal of and key to the Scriptures."[9]

THE HOLY SPIRIT AND SALVATION

The Holy Spirit is key in bringing the message of salvation in Jesus Christ to those whom the Spirit illumines and gives the gift of faith. We learn this message of Christ through the Scriptures, as God's written Word. The Spirit illumines us to believe the Scriptures are God's Word, the means God uses to make the gospel ("good news") of Jesus Christ known to us. Bullinger wrote: "For God himself alone, by sending his Holy Spirit into the hearts and minds of men, doth open our hearts, persuade our minds, and cause us with all our

8. Cochrane, ed., *Reformed Confessions*, 226.

9. Opitz, "Bullinger and Paul," in *Companion to Paul*, 258 n. 94. The Latin phrase is: "Christus finis et clavis scripturae."

heart to believe that which we by his word and teaching have learned to believe."[10] Our hearts and minds are opened by the Holy Spirit—to believe in Jesus Christ; and to believe in Scripture as the Word of God through which the message of Jesus Christ is made known to us. So, Bullinger urged: "Let us therefore beseech our Lord God to pour into our minds his holy Spirit, by whose virtue the seal of God's word may be quickened in our hearts, to the bringing forth of much fruit to the salvation of our souls, and the glory of God our Father. To whom be glory for ever."[11] We pray for God's Spirit to bring forth faith in Jesus Christ and in the Scriptures through which Christ becomes known to us.

Clearly, for Bullinger, "the cause or beginning of faith cometh not of any man, or any strength of man, but of God himself, who by his Holy Spirit inspireth faith into our hearts."[12] Salvation is wholly the work of God. As Bullinger put it: "We do not share in the benefit of justification [salvation] partly because of the grace of God or Christ, and partly because of ourselves, our love, works or merit, but we attribute it wholly to the grace of God in Christ through faith."[13] Bullinger wrote:

> This therefore is left unto us for a thing most certain and undoubtedly true, that true faith is the mere gift of God, which is by the Holy Ghost from heaven bestowed upon our minds, and is declared unto us in the word of truth by teachers

10. Bullinger, *Decades*, 1:85.

11. Bullinger, *Decades*, 1:70.

12. Bullinger, *Decades,* 1:84. Bullinger wrote that "The author of this regeneration is the Holy Ghost," *Decades*, 4:101. "Regeneration" means the "new birth" of coming to faith in Jesus Christ. Bullinger is referring here to John 3 and Jesus' words to Nicodemus: "Very truly, I tell you, no one can see the kingdom of God without being born from above" (John 3:3).

13. Cochrane, ed., *Reformed Confes*sions, 256–57.

sent of God, and is obtained by earnest prayers which cannot be tired. Whereby we learn, that we ought often and attentively to hear the word of God, and never cease to pray to God for the obtaining of true faith.[14]

Faith is the gift of God, given "by the Holy Spirit by means of the preaching of the Gospel and steadfast prayer."[15] The Spirit brings faith in Jesus Christ. Through the Holy Spirit, we receive forgiveness of sins and salvation in Jesus Christ: "The power, operation, or action of the Spirit is that, whatsoever the grace of God doth work in us through the Son."[16] We receive the grace of God in Jesus Christ by the work of the Holy Spirit, who brings us the gift of faith (Eph 2:8–9). This faith has power, not in and from itself, but by the power of the Holy Spirit: "Verily, the form of faith is engraven in the heart of the faithful by the Holy Ghost. And although it be small, and doth not grow up to the highest degree, yet notwithstanding it is true faith, having force in it as it were a grain of mustard-seed [see Luke 13:19]."[17]

The Spirit's work, in addition to initiating faith, is to sustain faith in Christ and enable believers in Christ to grow in faith and participate in sanctification. Bullinger wrote that "the Father indeed doth sanctify too, but by the blood of Jesus Christ, and poureth the same sanctification out of him into us by the Holy Ghost: so that it is, as it were, the property of the Holy Ghost to sanctify whereupon he is called Holy or the Sanctifier."[18] "For without him [the Holy Ghost]," wrote Bullinger, "there is no true sanctification."[19]

14. Bullinger, *Decades*, 1:87.
15. Cochrane, ed., *Reformed Confessions*, 257–58.
16. Bullinger, *Decades*, 1:156. On salvation, see chapter 7 below.
17. Bullinger, *Decades*, 1:101.
18. Bullinger, *Decades*, 1:155.
19. Bullinger, *Decades*, 1:156.

Believers receive the benefits of the work of Jesus Christ in bringing salvation and are sustained in their salvation by the ongoing work of the Holy Spirit. The Spirit enables believers to grow in grace and to serve God in Jesus Christ. This sanctification is enabled through the Spirit's grafting us into Christ and uniting us to Christ by faith. Bullinger used an interesting image to express this union with Christ: God pours "into us his Holy Spirit, the fulness of all good things; and doth communicate himself wholly to us, joining us unto himself with an indissoluble knot."[20] We are "tied together" with Jesus Christ by the power of the Holy Spirit. All through our lives, Christ lives in us, by the work of God's Holy Spirit.

Beyond the "knot" that ties together believers themselves with Jesus Christ, Bullinger saw union with the Holy Spirit as a mark of the Christian church in union with its Lord. For Bullinger: The Holy Spirit "couples" or unites

> the spouse of Christ with her spouse with a knot that cannot be loosed, and joineth together between themselves all the members of his mystical body in an everlasting covenant. For as the members of our body are joined together whole and sound by the benefit and enjoying of life, so the mystical body of Christ is united together by the Holy Ghost. Therefore it is no marvel that he is called or noted with the name of love, which poureth love into our hearts [Rom 5:5].[21]

This indissoluble bond of faith unites the whole church of Jesus Christ (the elect, in Bullinger's theology) to the Lord of the church, Jesus Christ (Eph 5:23). The bond, uniting all the members of the church to each other is the same bond of faith. This union with Christ by the church

20. Bullinger, *Decades*, 1:157.
21. Bullinger, *Decades*, 4:319.

and among the church's members is the Spirit's work of faith which is expressed by the love which the Spirit "pours into our hearts." These connections between Christ as head of the church and its members was captured succinctly by Bullinger in his *True Confession* (1545): "With the sole bond of the spirit and faith together with love, they are united with Christ and with each other as members of one body, sharing in the graces and gifts of their head and Saviour Christ."[22]

The graces given by the Holy Spirit to the church of Jesus Christ are many and varied. Throughout his writings, Bullinger mentions these often. In the largest sense, these include the "gifts of the Spirit" and all the church does, both within its own community and beyond, in the world. They also include the "good works" Christian believers do in service to God and as an expression of their faith in Jesus Christ, which is the means of their salvation. Bullinger said that

> we must pray continually, that the bountiful and liberal Lord will vouchsafe to bestow on us his Spirit, that by it the seal of God's word may be quickened in our heart, and that we, as holy and right hearers of his word right hearers of his word, may bear fruit abundantly to the glory of God, and the everlasting salvation of our own souls. For what will it avail to hear the word of God without faith, and without the Holy Spirit of God to work or stir inwardly in our hearts?[23]

The Holy Spirit leads us into good works, which are done "to the glory of God." These works express the Christian's faith and love for Jesus Christ—expressed, most often, for the benefit of other people. The motives for good works

22. Translated in Stephens, *Theology*, 159.
23. Bullinger, *Decades*, 1:66.

come from the Spirit and emerge from faith and love. Good works are ways by which true worship of God are expressed: "But God is truly worshipped, when we, ceasing from evil, and obeying God's holy Spirit, do exercise ourselves in the study of good works."[24] Good works are motivated by God's Spirit. They are ways by which the genuineness of Christian belief is shown in meaningful ways.

Christians should never mistakenly think, however, that good works are the basis of their salvation. This was a recurring emphasis of the Protestant reformers over against Roman Catholic views. Bullinger said in his Second Helvetic Confession: "Works ought not to be done in order that we may earn eternal life by them, for, as the apostle says, eternal life is the gift of God [Rom 6:23; Eph 2:8]."[25] Succinctly: "For we are freely saved, without respect of any works of ours, either first or last."[26]

Yet, Bullinger also notes that good works please God. Works proceed from faith. As the book of James puts it, "so faith by itself, if it has no works, is dead" (Jas 2:17). Christians express their faith by doing good works, which are "pleasing to God and are approved by him. Because of faith in Christ, those who do good works which, moreover, are done from God's grace through the Holy Spirit are pleasing to God."[27] Bullinger wrote: "And the works of faith are done of duty, although also of free accord; because we are created unto good works [Eph 5:19]. Yea, through Christ alone they do please and are acceptable to God the Father; for he is the vine, we are the branches. So all glory is reserved untouched to Christ alone: which is the surest note to know the true

---

24. Bullinger, *Decades*, 2:255.
25. Cochrane, ed., *Reformed Confessions*, 259.
26. Bullinger, *Decades*, 1:36.
27. Cochrane, ed., *Reformed Confessions*, 260.

gospel by."[28] Our faith leads us certainly, by the work of the Holy Spirit within us, to do works that serve God and serve others—the expression of our redemption and salvation in Christ. Through Christ, what his disciples do is pleasing and acceptable to God. In doing good works, Christ's people as "branches" are bringing the presence of the "vine"—Jesus Christ himself—to the world.

THE HOLY SPIRIT AND THE WORD

The Word of God incarnate is Jesus Christ—"the Word became flesh and lived among us" (John 1:14). God's Word written is Holy Scripture; and God's Word proclaimed is preaching (see chapter 2). The Holy Spirit is the means by which God's Word, in this threefold form, reaches us. Word and Spirit are inextricably bound up together. The Spirit witnesses to the Word, pointing to Jesus Christ, known to us through Scripture and preaching. The sacraments of the church are, for Bullinger, the seals of God's Word that strengthen our faith.

Bullinger wrote that "God doth by his Holy Spirit sanctify his faithful folk and constant believers: which he declareth unto the church by the preaching of the gospel, bearing witness thereunto and sealing it with his sacraments; so that he commandeth us with continual prayers incessantly to crave of him that glorious sanctification."[29] God's Holy Spirit works in believers to sanctify them—make them holy. This happens through the preaching of the Word of God and the witness of the sacraments—the ongoing ways the church is nurtured and believers are enabled to "grow in the grace and knowledge of our Lord and Savior Jesus Christ" (2 Pet 3:18). A constant prayer of Christian

28. Bullinger, *Decades*, 4:32.
29. Bullinger, *Decades*, 2:266.

believers is earnestly to desire this "glorious sanctification" that comes through God's Word through which they can grow in grace.

The outward ministry of God's Word is necessary as the means by which the gospel of Jesus Christ can be heard and believed. This accords with the teachings of Paul: "Faith comes from what is heard, and what is heard comes through the word of Christ" (Rom 10:17). Yet the "outer Word"—the proclamation of the gospel—must be met by the "inner Word"—the illumination of the Spirit of God. The inward Word (the power of God) is what moves people through the outward Word (the preaching of the gospel). Bullinger always wanted to emphasize Paul's conviction that it is "God who gives the growth" (1 Cor 3:7). The outward ministry of the Word is crucial for the church. But ultimately it is the Holy Spirit of God who confers faith, even as that faith comes by hearing the Word of God preached. Bullinger referred to Jesus' statement as key: "No one can come to me unless drawn by the Father who sent me" (John 6:44). Put another way: "external doctrine availeth nothing alone, unless inwardly, that is, in our hearts, we be moved by the Holy Spirit of our heavenly Father." We need, as Bullinger continued: "our ears to be pierced with the word of God, and our hearts touched with his Holy Spirit."[30]

The "outer word" must be met by the "inner word"—but the outer word must still be given. Preaching must happen; and the gospel of Jesus Christ must be proclaimed. Bullinger conveyed this in The Second Helvetic Confession, where he indicated that "inward illumination does not eliminate external preaching." God, who inwardly gives humans the Holy Spirit also, in Jesus, gave the commandment to preach the gospel to the whole creation (Mark 16:15) and Paul, in Philippi, "preached the Word outwardly

30. Bullinger, *Decades*, 4:59.

to Lydia, a seller of purple goods; but the Lord inwardly opened the woman's heart (Acts 16:14)."[31] Ultimately, again: "Faith comes from what is heard, and what is heard comes through the word of Christ" (Rom 10:17).

At the same time, said Bullinger, "we recognize that God can illuminate whom and when he will, even without the external ministry, for that is in his power; but we speak of the usual way of instructing men, delivered unto us from God, both by commandment and examples."[32] Preaching is not useless because of the need for the inward illumination of the Spirit. Preaching the Word is necessary for faith to be given to people by the Holy Spirit. The same God, who gives the gift of faith by the work of the Spirit is also the God who commands the outward preaching of the Word. This is God's usual pattern. Bullinger holds together the work of God through God's Word and God's Spirit.

All in all, Bullinger could write: "For the children of God are not born of flesh and blood, but from heaven, by the renewing of the Holy Spirit, who through the preaching of God's word planteth faith in our hearts, by which faith we are made the true members of Christ and his church."[33]

THE HOLY SPIRIT AND THE SACRAMENTS

In the Protestant tradition, just as Word and Spirit go together, so do Word and sacraments. This is certainly true for Bullinger. The Word of God comes to us in preaching. It also comes through the sacraments.

In Protestantism, there are two sacraments: baptism and the Lord's Supper. This is in contrast to the Roman Catholic tradition in which there are seven sacraments. A

---

31. Cochrane, ed., *Reformed Confes*sions, 225.
32. Cochrane, ed., *Reformed Confes*sions, 225.
33. Bullinger, *Decades*, 5:26.

main theological insight of the Protestant Reformers is that the sacraments are to be received *in faith*, which, is the gift of God, given through the Holy Spirit. Sacraments are efficacious, or effective, when they are received in faith. Some have called sacraments "the visible words of God." The sacraments are visible signs of an invisible grace, as Augustine said. The outward forms of the sacraments: water, in baptism; and the bread and wine in the Lord's Supper, point to an inward reality: what the sacraments mean, theologically.

Bullinger, like Zwingli before him, developed a view of the sacraments that did not completely agree with the beliefs of other Reformers, especially John Calvin.[34] Important here in relation to Bullinger's views of the Holy Spirit is to recognize the role of the Spirit in the sacraments. Word and Sacraments go together—and are joined together by the work of the Holy Spirit. As Bullinger put it, quoting Zwingli: "For the Lord speaketh, and the elements also speak; and they speak and persuade that to our senses, which the word and Spirit speaketh to our mind. Howbeit, hitherto all these visible things are nothing, unless the sanctification of the Spirit go before."[35]

Bullinger is clear the sacraments are instituted by God: "Surely the Lord himself instituted and put in use the sacraments."[36] For "the sacraments do serve to seal and represent to us the mysteries of Christ."[37] The sacraments carry out an important function: "The sacraments do testify the remission of sins and the heavenly gifts prepared for all them that do believe in Jesus Christ."[38] Or also: "For with

34. For a discussion of Bullinger's views on the sacrament, see chapter 9, below.

35. Bullinger, *Decades*, 5:332.

36. Bullinger, *Decades*, 4:228.

37. Bullinger, *Decades*, 4:32.

38. Bullinger, *Decades*, 4:89.

Holy Spirit

his grace he calleth, with the blood of Christ he purifieth; that which he sheweth by his word to be received by faith, and sealeth with sacraments, that the faithful should doubt of nothing touching their salvation obtained through Christ."[39] Further, "the outward marks and tokens of the church are the word and the sacrament. For these bring us into the society of one ecclesiastical body, and keep us in the same."[40]

Through it all, most important too is that in both Word and sacrament, it is the work of the Holy Spirit that is necessary for Word and sacrament to be effective. Without the Spirit bringing faith, God's Word and Sacraments have no power. Bullinger said:

> When faith, the gift of the Holy Ghost, goeth before, the sealing of the sacraments is very strong and sure. Some also have said very well: If our minds be destitute of the Holy Ghost, the sacraments do no more profit us, than it doth a blind man to look upon the bright beams of the sun. But if our eyes be opened through the illumination of the Spirit, they are wonderfully delighted with the heavenly sight of the sacraments.[41]

The sacraments are gifts of God. They are received in faith, as the work of the Holy Spirit. As Bullinger said in The Second Helvetic Confession, "the value of the sacraments depends upon faith and upon the truthfulness and pure goodness of God."[42] The Spirit's work of generating faith provides the means by which sacraments fulfill one of their functions, according to Bullinger: God, "strengthens

---

39. Bullinger, *Decades*, 5:17
40. Bullinger, *Decades*, 5:19.
41. Bullinger, *Decades*, 5:326. Cf. 5:273.
42. Cochrane, ed., *Reformed Confessions*, 281.

and increases our faith through the working of God's Spirit in our hearts."[43]

THE HOLY SPIRIT

While the Holy Spirit does not "stand out" in Bullinger's theology, the Spirit clearly plays a very important role in his thought. The Spirit enables many things to happen—in the world, in the church, and in the lives of Christian believers. So Bullinger actually has a robust doctrine of the Spirit, who "stands behind" important theological topics such as the Trinity, Scripture, salvation, Word, and sacrament.

The Holy Spirit dramatizes how important the divine work is prior to human activities and how Christian faith depends on God's initiative throughout the course of all creation and human life. As a member of the Trinity, the Spirit participates in the full activities of God. One of the theological understandings emerging from the early church was that the work of one member of the Trinity is also the work of the other members of the Trinity as well. God is "one God in three persons." All the persons participate fully in the Godhead. So the work of God the Father and God the Son is also the work of God the Holy Spirit. This means there is a pervasiveness to the Spirit's activities of which we may not be much aware most of the time.

Yet the Spirit is there, undergirding and sustaining all God does in creation, in salvation, and in the lives of God's people who live by faith and carry out good works through the Spirit's work within them.

The lives of God's people are strengthened and enriched by God's Word in Holy Spirit. The Spirit inspired Scripture and continues to interpret Scripture to believers.

43. Cochrane, ed., *Reformed Confessions*, 277.

Holy Spirit

God's people receive the gift of salvation in Jesus Christ. The Holy Spirit brings the gift of faith, which is the means by which salvation is received.

The people of God are sustained in their lives by continually listening to God's Word through preaching. The Spirit of God enables preaching to be meaningful in the lives of those who hear it in faith.

For Bullinger, a way God strengthens the faith of God's people is through the sacraments: baptism and the Lord's Supper. It is the Spirit who makes the sacraments effective for believers as they grow in grace by the ongoing work of the Holy Spirit in their lives.

In all these ways—and more—God's Holy Spirit is active and at work. In this sense, all the goodness and blessings believers receive may be attributed to the work of God's Holy Spirit. Best of all, as Bullinger reminds: "God is joined unto us by his Spirit; and we are coupled to him by faith, through the gift of the Holy Ghost."[44] This means also that "we are knit invisibly with Christ and all his members by unity of faith and participation of one Spirit."[45] The Holy Spirit works!

QUESTIONS FOR DISCUSSION

1. Why do you think the Holy Spirit has been underemphasized as a member of the Trinity by some people?

2. In what ways do you think the Holy Spirit helps us interpret Scripture today?

3. Theologically, why was it important for Bullinger and others to emphasize that the gift of faith in Jesus Christ is given by the Holy Spirit?

44. Bullinger, *Decades*, 5:309.
45. Bullinger, *Decades*, 5:467.

4. What were Bullinger's views about ways the Holy Spirit was active in relation to preaching; and with the sacraments?

6

PREDESTINATION AND COVENANT

Two key theological themes that have been important in Reformed theology are predestination (also called "election") and covenant. Reformed theologians have seen both as being firmly and clearly taught in Scripture. Theological developments of these biblical ideas have been based on the need for Christian people to have clear understandings of what these biblical teachings mean in relation to the whole of Christian theology. Both these doctrines have far-reaching implications for understanding who God is, what God does, and how God relates to human beings.

Sometimes Reformed theology and some Reformed theologians have been said to have made predestination a "central dogma" or "doctrine" from which they derive other doctrines. This characterization is not accurate since the Reformed emphasize that the fullness of God's being and God's works, "the whole purpose of God" (Acts 20:27), is what is to be understood and be the basis for theological knowledge. Predestination takes its place in that wider context. Likewise, Reformed theology has sometimes been called "covenant theology." This is a way of indicating that the concept or motif of covenant has been an important way of viewing the Scriptures as a whole and of understanding God's way of relating to or connecting with people—corporately (as with Israel in the Old Testament; and the church in the New Testament) and individually.[1]

Predestination and covenant are important theological concepts. This is so, especially, for Heinrich Bullinger. He wrote a good deal on predestination and devoted a chapter to it in his Second Helvetic Confession. It is also clear that "covenant" was important to Bullinger, so much so that it is sometimes said that this was the organizing principle of Bullinger's theology. Not all scholars agree with this assessment. But there is no doubt that covenant was a significant theological theme that helped shape Bullinger's reading and understanding of Scripture.

PREDESTINATION

The issue of predestination has always raised a number of theological questions. It has been controversial since the days of the early church and the theological debates in which Augustine defended the doctrine against those who wanted to emphasize human actions in relation to salvation instead of the primary actions of God.

---

1. The Latin term for "covenant" is *testamentum*. Thus we have the "Old Testament" and "New Testament," which can also be understood as "Old Covenant" and "New Covenant." "Covenant theology" views all Scripture as focused on "covenant" as the Bible's central theme. As one scholar noted, "Bullinger followed Zwingli in seeing in the Bible and the church's history one long story of God's covenant relationship with humankind." See Wallace, Jr., "Federal Theology," 136.

Predestination and Covenant

Predestination or election refer to God's choosing persons to whom the gift of faith is given, by the work of the Holy Spirit, and through which they receive eternal salvation. "Elect" has been the term used (Mark 13:20; Rom 8:33; Titus 1:1) for those who have received the gift of salvation by God's gracious election or predestination in Jesus Christ. God's choosing a people is in order for them to receive the benefits of salvation and also to carry out God's purposes in the world (1 Thess 1:4; 2 Pet 1:10). A passage from Romans has been especially important for the Reformed: "We know that all things work together for good for those who love God, who are called according to his purpose. For those whom he foreknew he also predestined to be conformed to the image of his Son, in order that he might be the firstborn within a large family. And those whom he predestined he also called; and those whom he called he also justified; and those whom he justified he also glorified" (Rom 8:28–30).

Heinrich Bullinger was committed to teaching and proclaiming God's election or predestination as a key understanding of God's will and work. Zwingli, Bullinger's friend and predecessor in Zurich, had also taught predestination.[2] Bullinger defended Zwingli's views, but also went on to develop the doctrine in his own ways. Bullinger believed the doctrine was taught in Scripture but also that it must be handled with care so misconceptions or misinterpretations did not cause difficulties for the faith of believers in the church. Bullinger wanted to treat the doctrine with pastoral concern and sensitivity.[3]

---

2. Zwingli's preferred term was "election" whereas Bullinger used "predestination." In the Second Helvetic Confession, however, predestination and election are used synonymously.

3. Bullinger referred to some issues that relate to predestination as "curious questions" in his Second Helvetic Confession. See Cochrane, ed., *Reformed Confes*sions, 237. He wanted to avoid being "overly speculative" about predestination. Muller notes that Bullinger's stress

This concern that predestination be a doctrine of comfort and good hope for people of faith is seen clearly in Bullinger's presentation "Of the Predestination of God and the Election of the Saints" in his Second Helvetic Confession.[4] His first point—and a strong emphasis of all the Protestant reformers—is that God has elected us *out of grace*. This means God's acts of predestination and election to bring salvation are solely the work of God; and done out of God's pure grace and love. Bullinger wrote:

> From eternity God has freely, and of his mere grace, without any respect to men, predestinated or elected the saints whom he will to save in Christ, according to the saying of the apostle, "God chose us in him before the foundation of the world" (Eph. 1:4). And again; "Who saved us and called us with a holy calling not in virtue of our works but in virtue of his own purpose and the grace which he gave us in Christ Jesus ages ago, and now has manifested through the appearing of our Savior Jesus Christ" (II Tim. 1:9f.).

These scriptural passages show that salvation is by God's grace, and the will of God is to save persons "in Christ" apart from any human activities or actions. Salvation is, as Luther emphasized, by grace alone!

God's grace comes to the elect, those chosen by God, in and through Jesus Christ. The Holy Spirit brings the gift of faith for persons to believe in Jesus Christ as the one who died for their sins, their Lord and Savior (Rom 5:8; 1 Cor

---

is less on God's decree than on "its execution in time"—in "covenant" as an expression of God's "eternally gracious will." See Muller, *Christ and the Decree*, 43.

4. The following quotations from chapter 10 of The Second Helvetic Confession come from Cochrane, ed., *Reformed Confessions*, 240–42.

12:3). Salvation by God's grace means, said Bullinger: "Although not on account of any merit of ours, God has elected us, not directly, but in Christ, and on account of Christ, in order that those who are now ingrafted into Christ by faith might also be elected." Salvation is by God's grace through faith in Jesus Christ. Those who are "ingrafted into Christ by faith" are those whom God has elected and chosen to be God's people and receive the gift of salvation. "Those who were outside Christ," said Bullinger, were "rejected" (citing 2 Cor 13:5). Jesus Christ is the one who died to provide salvation. Those who are "outside Christ"—who have no love for Christ or desire to serve Christ—are cut off from salvation. By their own actions, in choosing not to live for Christ, they live for themselves and thus are outside the salvation Christ brings.

There is no "merit" humans can claim in obtaining salvation. Salvation is God's gift, given to the elect for a definite purpose. Bullinger wrote: "The saints are chosen in Christ by God for a definite purpose, which the apostle himself explains when he says, 'He chose us in him for adoption that we should be holy and blameless before him in love.'" God destined us to be adopted into the family of God "through Jesus Christ" that we "should be to the praise of the glory of his grace" (Eph 1:4ff.). The purpose of election is for the elect to live in love—as we know from the Scriptures: to love God and to love others (Mark 12:30–31). We are "adopted"—a theological term used especially by Paul (Rom 8:15; Eph 1:5)—to speak of our being brought into the family of God, the people of God: so we can live for the "praise of the glory of his grace." The purpose of the elect, of those chosen by God, is to live for the glory of God, praising God's grace. We live for the glory of God when we serve God in love. As an old saying goes: "We are not saved to sit; we are saved to serve." Our lives have purpose and direction in glorifying God.

This leads Bullinger to say we are to have a good hope for all people. The elect are not to gloat or glory in their election. They are rather to hope the same grace and faith given to them will be extended to others—to all others. Said Bullinger: "Although God knows who are his, and here and there mention is made of the small number of the elect, yet we must hope well of all, and not rashly judge any man to be a reprobate" (see Phil 1:3–7). "Reprobates" are those who do not receive salvation and remain in their sins. God's people are to hope God's election and the gift of faith are extended to others. It is not the prerogative of the elect to decide and declare who are those who will not be saved by God (reprobate). God is free. God acts according to God's divine will. Election and predestination, along with the giving of the gift of faith by the Holy Spirit, is solely the work of God. It is not for God's people to speculate about who will or will not receive God's election and salvation.

God's gracious election and predestination along with the good hope for all is the strongest impetus for preaching the gospel to all people. Since Christians cannot "rashly judge" anyone "to be a reprobate," the imperative is to preach the gospel of God's love in Jesus Christ to all creation and "make disciples of all nations" (Matt 28:19). Christians are not to speculate about the salvation of others; they are to proclaim the gospel of God's grace so the Holy Spirit can bring others to faith so, as Bullinger said, "those who are now ingrafted into Christ by faith might also be elected." God's election and predestination propel the people of God to "Go into all the world and proclaim the good news to the whole creation" (Mark 16:15).

The blessings of God's election and predestination bring with them responsibilities and the need for self-examination and obedience to God's will and way for the elect. To the question of whether few are elect, Bullinger put the obligation on believers: Jesus "exhorts every man to 'strive to enter by the narrow door' (Luke 13:24): as if he should say, It is not for you curiously to inquire about these matters, but rather to endeavor that you may enter into heaven by the straight way." Election brings responsibilities, to live in love and glorify God by serving God and others in Jesus Christ.

Election should not promote careless and selfish living. Bullinger wrote that "we do not approve of the impious speeches of some who say, 'Few are chosen, and since I do not know whether I am among the number of the few, I will enjoy myself.' Likewise, some may say that 'if I am in the number of the reprobate, no faith or repentance will help me, since the decree of God cannot be changed. Therefore all doctrines and admonitions are useless.'" Since we never know when or where faith may be granted by the Holy Spirit to those who have not yet come to faith, preaching must continue and admonitions to come to faith must always be given.

When it comes to the question of whether we are elected, Bullinger's answer is simple: "For the preaching of the Gospel is to be heard, and it is to be believed; and it is to be held as beyond doubt that if you believe and are in Christ you are elected. For the Father has revealed unto us in Christ the eternal purpose of his predestination" (citing 2 Tim 1:9–10). God, in Christ, invites all to come to Christ: "Come to me all who labor and are heavy-laden, and I will give you rest" (Matt 11:28). The promise of the gospel is: "For God so loved the world that he gave his only Son, so that everyone who believes in him may not perish but may have eternal life" (John 3:16).

Bullinger's christological focus in predestination continues when he writes: "Let Christ, therefore be the looking glass, in whom we may contemplate our predestination.

We shall have a sufficiently clear and sure testimony that we are inscribed in the Book of Life if we have fellowship with Christ, and he is ours and we are his in true faith."[5] So, if you want to know if you are "elect," ask yourself: "Do I believe in Jesus Christ?" For it is in Christ we see the one in whom God's election is made clear. If we have "fellowship with Christ, and he is ours"—we are in "true faith" and are of the elect of God. As Bullinger had written earlier, "if thou hast communion or fellowship with Christ, thou art predestinate to life, and thou art of the number of the elect and chosen."[6] "Faith therefore," said Bullinger, "is a most assured sign that thou art elected; and whiles thou art called to the communion of Christ, and art taught faith, the most loving God declareth towards thee his election and good-will."[7] So, "let us keep it deeply printed in our breasts, that God hath chosen us in Christ, and for Christ his sake predestinate us to life."[8]

---

5. Cochrane, ed., *Reformed Confessions*, 242. John Calvin also used the image of the "mirror" ("looking glass"—Bullinger) when he called Jesus Christ "the mirror wherein we must, and without self-deception may, contemplate our own election." See Calvin, *Institutes*, 3.24.5.

6. Bullinger, *Decades*, 4:187. Bullinger mentions 1 John 5:12: "Whoever has the Son has life; whoever does not have the Son of God does not have life." Cf. Eph 1:4–7. Bullinger does not delve into "double predestination"—a positive and negative predestination: to life (elect) and to death (reprobate). Bullinger associates the will of God with election to life in Jesus Christ. Condemnation by God comes to those who reject Christ and are outside Christ. Bullinger points away from what is not known and toward what is known to us from Scripture.

7. Bullinger, *Decades*, 4:187.

8. Bullinger, *Decades*, 4:192.

COVENANT

God's eternal election in Jesus Christ and the ingrafting of a people to be God's people is expressed in history through God's covenants. Predestination and covenant are closely related in God's work of salvation.[9] Covenant is a central concept for Bullinger, found throughout his writings, though—strangely enough—it does not have a separate chapter in Bullinger's Second Helvetic Confession.

God's covenant of grace is given by God's initiative and is a way for persons to understand and experience what God wants to do in providing salvation. Bullinger wrote that "God, in making of leagues, as he doth in all things else, applieth himself to our capacities, and imitateth the order which men use in making confederacies."[10] God accommodates God's self to human capacities (as with the Scriptures themselves) to give humans an example so they can understand what God wills and wants to do. In the human realm, God uses what humans use in their lives and societies—they form bonds and associations with each other. As Bullinger put it, humans "bind themselves to the society and fellowship of one body or people." In a "covenant," God is doing the same: "And therefore, when God's mind was to declare the favour and good-will that he bare to mankind, and to make us men partakers wholly of himself and his goodness, by pouring himself out upon us, to our great good and profit, it pleased him to make a league or covenant with mankind." God wanted to express "favour and good-will" to humans. So God established covenants to express what God wanted to convey.

---

9. Venema writes that "election calls for covenant and renders it effective as an instrument of salvation." See Venema, *Doctrine*, 119.

10. Bullinger, *Decades*, 3:169.

Covenants define relationships. They express the commitments of the one who initiates the covenant. Covenants may be unilateral—in which one party (God) makes promises that humans simply receive. God promised Abraham: "I will make my covenant between me and you, and will make you exceedingly numerous" (Gen 17:2) and "I will establish my covenant between me and you, and your offspring after you throughout their generations, for an everlasting covenant, to be God to you and to your offspring after you" (Gen 17:7). Abraham received what God—by grace—promised to him.

A covenant may be bilateral—in which God makes promises and stipulations; and humans respond by obeying and seeking to fulfill the conditions of the covenant. In the covenant at Sinai, God told Moses to say to the people of Israel: "Now therefore, if you obey my voice and keep my covenant, you shall be my treasured possession out of all the peoples. Indeed, the whole earth is mine, but you shall be for me a priestly kingdom and a holy nation" (Gen 19:5). Then Moses received the Ten Commandments and the people of Israel had concrete instruction about what it would mean to be God's covenant people and how the covenant could be kept. The people were to live in obedience as a "holy nation" for receiving the gift of God as their God and being God's "treasured possession out of all the peoples."

Throughout the Bible, God establishes covenants with the people of God. Bullinger traces the line of God's covenants in the Old Testament: with Adam—to receive blessedness. This is grounded in God's prophetic promise (Gen 3:15); to Noah—as a statement of God's promise (Gen 6:18; 9:16–17); to Abraham—to establish God's people (Gen 17:2, 4, 7); and to Moses—"written in the two tables"—(the

Ten Commandments; Exod 20:1–17) as Bullinger said, with "many ceremonies added thereunto."[11]

But all the covenants of the Old Testament are fulfilled in Jesus Christ. The older, former covenants have now been superseded and made complete in God's sending Jesus Christ to die for human sin and provide the "new covenant" (1 Cor 11:25) which forever expresses God's love and forgiveness and which is the means of eternal salvation. Said Bullinger: "This is the new covenant that God in his Christ hath made with us, 'that he will not remember our iniquities' (Heb. 8:12)."[12] Bullinger wrote:

> But most excellently of all, most clearly and evidently, did our Lord and Saviour Jesus Christ himself shew forth that league; who, wiping away all the ceremonies, types, figures, and shadows, brought in instead of them the very truth, and did most absolutely fulfil and finish the old league, bringing all the principles of our salvation and true godliness into a brief summary, which, for the renewing and fulfilling of all things, and for the abrogation of the old ceremonies, he called the new league, or new testament. In that testament Christ alone is preached, the perfectness and fulness of all things; in it there is nothing more desired than faith and charity; and in it is granted holy and wonderful liberty unto the godly.[13]

Jesus Christ is the fulfillment of God's covenant of grace with the people of Israel and is God's giving of God's own self, in Christ, so God's grace is extended to those whom God has elected and chosen to be the people of God.

---

11. Bullinger, *Decades*, 3:169.
12. Bullinger, *Decades*, 1:110.
13. Bullinger, *Decades*, 3:169–70.

Christ's work of salvation is the historical goal of God's covenant promises, given throughout the Old Testament.

In all God's covenant relationships, Bullinger affirms the initiation of the covenant is with God and covenants are expressions of God's grace. Salvation is from God in Jesus Christ through the work of the Holy Spirit. This is the theological understanding that glorifies God. Bullinger said that in salvation, "we will have all glory to be ascribed unto God."[14] Human responsibility in receiving God's covenantal gift of grace in Jesus Christ is expressed in the lives of those who have received salvation by God's grace (justification). They seek to live in obedience to God's will and ways (sanctification) in response to God's gracious salvation. As Bullinger said, "God is always the God of his people: he doth always demand and require of them faithful obedience."[15]

Part of this obedience is obeying God's law. God's law expresses God's will. Those who have received God's covenant of grace in Jesus Christ seek to follow God's will and way for living by obeying the law of God. They obey from gratitude for God's grace in Christ. Bullinger makes it clear that a person "is not justified by the works of the law, but by faith in Christ Jesus."[16] Faith is not what we do; it is what God does. Faith is a gift of God (Eph 2:8). As Bullinger says: "This faith is not of me, but is the mere gift of God, by the Holy Ghost."[17] Salvation and the good works of obedience flowing from salvation are by faith, the gift of God.

Circumcision was given to Abraham as the sign of the covenant (Gen 17:9–14). This action signified inclusion into God's covenant people. Bullinger wrote that "circumcision did signify and testify that God Almighty, of his mere

14. Bullinger, *Common-places*, V,8, (p. 144).
15. Bullinger, *Decades*, 3:170.
16. Bullinger, *Common-places* , V,1 (p. 104).
17. Bullinger, *Common-places*, VI,1 (p. 118).

grace and goodness, is joined with an indissoluble bond of covenant unto us men, whom his will is first to sanctify, then to justify and lastly to enrich with all heavenly treasures through Christ, our Lord and reconciler."[18] The physical act of circumcision was a means of signifying and testifying to God's grace and goodness in establishing a bond with humans—with Abraham and his posterity. This bond was a covenant of grace, which established Abraham and his offspring as God's own people. Later, God promised Israel would be "my treasured possession out of all the peoples" (Gen 19:5). Bullinger recognized that as God accommodated the divine intentions to human capacities for understanding, the physical action pointed toward the theological reality of God's covenant of grace.

God's way of providing a physical "sign" of a theological reality became a basis for Bullinger's understanding of the nature of the sacraments.[19] In relation to covenant, Bullinger recognized "the two sacraments of the old church, circumcision and the Passover."[20] These correspond to the Protestant understanding of the two New Testament "sacraments" instituted by Jesus: baptism and the Lord's Supper. Bullinger wrote: "The sacraments also of the ancient Jews are flatly abrogated, and in their places are substituted new sacraments, which are given the people of the new covenant. Instead of circumcision is baptism appointed [Gal 5:2–4] and . . . instead of the paschal Lamb is the Lord's supper ordained, which by another name is called the eucharist, or a thanksgiving."[21]

Now, in Jesus Christ, the old "sacraments" or "signs" are fulfilled and superseded. Now, Christ "doth spiritually

18. Bullinger, *Decades*, 3:174.

19. On Bullinger's views on the sacraments, see ch. 9 below.

20. Bullinger, *Decades*, 3:217.

21. Bullinger, *Decades*, 3:269.

circumcise the faithful, and hath given them instead of circumcision the sacrament of baptism."²² The physical reality of circumcision is now replaced by the institution of baptism. Theologically, Jesus Christ is "the fulfilling and perfectness of the law and the prophets."²³ Jesus Christ himself is the "new covenant" (1 Cor 11:25). In Jesus Christ, God's people are established as the church. They receive God's covenant of grace in the person of Jesus, who is "the mediator of a new covenant, so that those who are called may receive the promised eternal inheritance, because a death has occurred that redeems them from the transgressions under the first covenant" (Heb 9:15).

Bullinger saw Christ as uniting those who received God's covenant of grace, in him: "For even so did Christ take away circumcision, the sacrifices, and all the ceremonies, to the end that of the Jews and Gentiles he might make one church and fellowship."²⁴ For, "we the believers of the new covenant, are one church and one people, which are all saved under one congregation, under one only testament, and by one and the same manner of means, to wit, by faith in Christ Jesu."²⁵ Now, in Jesus Christ, Jews and gentiles are joined in the one covenant of God who is Jesus Christ himself.²⁶ By faith, believers in Jesus Christ receive the benefits

22. Bullinger, *Decades*, 3:249.

23. Bullinger, *Decades*, 3:249.

24. Bullinger, *Decades*, 3:259.

25. Bullinger, *Decades*, 3:293

26. In Bullinger's theology Jesus Christ is himself the covenant, the agreement between God and humankind. He is both God and man, and thus perfectly brings the two parties, the divine and the human, together. All God's covenant promises from the Old Testament onward are fulfilled in Jesus Christ and what he did in his death on the cross. We see this in Jesus' words at the Last Supper: 'This cup that is poured out for you is the new covenant in my blood" (Luke 22:20). Jesus himself is the covenant. As some theologians have put it, "Jesus

of the new covenant in him: "The people of the new covenant, are freely disburdened and set at liberty. And he by whom we are disburdened is Jesus Christ, in whom alone we have all things necessary to life and salvation."[27]

While Bullinger did not devote a chapter to covenant in The Second Helvetic Confession, he did mention it in significant ways in his chapter "Of Holy Baptism."[28] There he spoke of the institution of baptism and Jesus' command to baptize "in the name of the Father and of the Son and of the Holy Spirit (Matt. 28:19)" and baptism in the earliest church (Acts 2:37f.).

For Bullinger, baptism is a sign of participating in the covenant of God—the covenant of grace, now made clear in Jesus Christ. He wrote: "To be baptized in the name of Christ is to be enrolled, entered, and received into the covenant and family, and so into the inheritance of the [children] of God" (see Eph 1:14; 1 Pet 1:4). Baptism expresses one's new status and identity in the covenantal "family" of God and the "inheritance" one receives as God's children. Here it is clear Bullinger was emphasizing God's enabling persons to be drawn into God's people through a relationship of faith with Jesus Christ.

Christ is the substance of the covenant." The word "covenant" means "promise." As Paul said, in Jesus Christ "every one of God's promises is a 'Yes'" (2 Cor 1:20). In the person and work of Jesus Christ, all God's covenants and covenant promises are real!

27. Bullinger, *Decades*, 3:296. Bullinger went on to say that "Christ is the fulfilling of all the types and ceremonies; by whose Spirit since we do now possess the thing prefigured, we have no longer need of the representing types and shadows. The external things that Christ hath ordained are very few, and of very small cost. Therefore the people of the new testament doth enjoy a passing great and ample liberty."

28. See Cochrane, ed., *Reformed Confessions*, 282–83 from which the following quotations are taken.

In this, the baptized are "granted the manifold grace of God, in order to lead a new and innocent life." God's gift of grace is given so those baptized are a "new creation," as Paul said (2 Cor 5:17) and are enabled (by the work of the Holy Spirit) to experience new life in relationship with God in Jesus Christ.

Baptism is God's action—through the church—as a sign of being cleansed "from the filthiness of sins" and being new persons in Christ.[29] Bullinger said: "Baptism, therefore, calls to mind and renews the great favor God has shown to the race of mortal men." Baptism is a sign of the covenant of God's grace—"the great favor God has shown" to human sinners. God "who is rich in mercy, freely cleanses us from our sins by the blood of his Son, and in him adopts us" into God's family." Then God, "by a holy covenant joins us to himself, and enriches us with various gifts, that we might live a new life. All these things are assured by baptism." God's "holy covenant" in Jesus Christ joins the baptized to God who gives "gifts" so we can live a new life. This is what baptism points toward!

"Inwardly," said Bullinger, "we are regenerated, purified, and renewed by God through the Holy Spirit." The Spirit works to make us new persons in Jesus Christ. "Outwardly," Bullinger wrote, "we receive the assurance of the greatest gifts in the water, by which also those great benefits are represented, and, as it were, set before our eyes to be beheld." God's covenant of grace is in Jesus Christ and the benefits believers receive are represented in the action of baptism and clearly "set before our eyes to be beheld." Baptism points to the work of God's Spirit, who points to Jesus Christ himself!

While baptism is a one-time act, for Bullinger, the sign of baptism—pointing to God's promise—is lifelong and

---

29. Bullinger also wrote: "Baptism is a sign, a testimony and sealing, of our cleansing," *Decades*, 5:397.

lasting. This is because baptism points to God's covenant of grace, now the "new covenant" in Jesus Christ. So Bullinger encouraged:

> For the promise of God is true. The seal of the promise is true, not deceivable. The power of Christ is ever effectual throughly [*sic,* thoroughly] to cleanse and wash away all the sins of them that be his. How often therefore soever we have sinned in our life-time, let us call into our remembrance the mystery of holy baptism; wherewith for the whole course of our life we are washed that we might know, and not doubt, that our sins are forgiven us of the same God and our Lord, yea, and by the blood of Christ, into whom by baptism once we are graffed [grafted], that he might always work salvation in us, even till we be received out of misery into glory.[30]

God's covenant promise of grace, known in Jesus Christ, is true; and to be remembered in remembering one's baptism.

QUESTIONS FOR DISCUSSION

1. In what ways have your views about predestination been affected—if at all—by realizing how Bullinger understood this doctrine?

2. Why did Bullinger's views of predestination provide a basis for preaching the gospel to all people and holding out good hope for all people?

3. Why is it valuable for Bullinger to teach that we should contemplate election by looking at Jesus Christ?

4. In what ways was God's covenant of grace important in Bullinger's theology?

30. Bullinger, *Decades*, 5:398.

7

SIN AND SALVATION

Heinrich Bullinger had a profoundly lively understanding of sin, the fall of mankind, the inability of the law to make fallen men and women right with God, and the means of justification.[1] Early in his career he sporadically discussed the issues to which we now turn. But he did not offer any sustained argument on the subjects of sin, fall, and restoration until his sermons collected in the *Decades*.

Nonetheless, his sporadic mentions of these doctrines do contain the kernels of his thought and the substance of the ideas that he would later develop more fully. So, for instance, his lectures on Romans and his responses to the Anabaptists both contain nascent doctrine. But, again, it is not until the *Decades* and his little systematic theology titled "The Christian Religion" that he provides the interested with full treatments of these teachings. Accordingly, we will focus our attention in what follows on those texts.

1. See Stephens' *Theology*, 225–92.

SIN AND THE FALL

Bullinger preached on sin in the tenth sermon of the Third *Decade*. Here he describes original sin, actual sin, the sin against the Holy Spirit, and the punishment for sin. Bullinger begins this wonderful sermon, after asking his hearers to pray for him while he preaches, with the following declaration:

> Sin is of most men taken for error; for that, I mean, whereby we do not only err from the thing which is true, right, just and good, but do also follow and decline to that which is naught. The Latins derive their word peccatum, sin, of pellicatus, whore-hunting; which is a fault of wedded people that are corrupted with the spirit of fornication, as when men prefer harlots before their lawful wives. And this definition, verily, doth wonderfully agree to this present treatise.[2]

The power of sin over the lives of its victims has been the most destructive force in history. Sin effaces everything that it touches. It violates all goodness and actually has the power to so injure the image of God in humanity that humankind no longer bears the image of God in any meaningful sense, until regenerated. Sin's power to destroy is made most apparent in the fact that people die. But illness, disaster, divorce, war, poverty, famine, injustice, and all the other ills people experience all have their roots in sin. Sin is a poison that has spread through all humanity. It is a disease that infects everyone, from the moment of conception till the last breath is drawn. It is not mere error, or "a mistake." It is a willful act of rebellion, of contempt for God. But where does it come from?

---

2. Bullinger, *Decades*, 3:358.

Bullinger stringently rejects the idea that sin has its origins in the will of God, as though God would wish the ill of his creatures. God is also not the author of sin in any person. Neither, Bullinger insists, is the devil the author of our sin. He can tempt, he can provoke, but he cannot *cause* men and women to sin. That decision is wholly within their power. Bullinger opines:

> He hath, I confess, great subtilties, and more than rhetorical force, wherewith to persuade us: but God is stronger, and never ceaseth to prompt good and wholesome counsels unto the souls of his faithful servants. Neither doth he permit more to Satan than is for our commodity: as is to be seen in the example of that holy man, the patient Job; and also in the example of Paul, 2 Cor. 12, and in his words, saying, "God is faithful, which will not suffer us to be tempted above that we are able to bear." They therefore are vainly seduced, which cast the fault of their sin upon the devil's shoulders.[3]

If Satan is not the direct cause of sin, what is? Bullinger blames man's will and Satan's wiles. Or to be more precise:

> sin doth spring not of God, which hateth and doth prohibit all evil, but of the devil; the free election of our grand-parents and their corrupted will, which was depraved by the devil's lie, and the false shew of feigned good. So then the devil and the yielding or corrupted mind of man are the very causes of sin and naughtiness.[4]

Yielding to Satan gave birth to sin. And that sin infected all humans through their parents. Here, naturally, Bullinger, along with the rest of the Reformers, simply followed

3. Bullinger, *Decades*, 3:362–63.
4. Bullinger, *Decades*, 3:370.

Augustine's teaching that sin is passed down from the father through his seed to children at their conception. The diseased root cannot but infect every branch with disease.

In the Second Helvetic Confession, chapter 8, Bullinger expresses precisely what he means when he talks about sin, and its causes and consequences. He writes of original sin:

> We therefore acknowledge that original sin is in all men; we acknowledge that all other sins which spring therefrom are both called and are indeed sins, by what name soever they may be termed, whether mortal or venial, or also that which is called sin against the Holy Spirit, which is never forgiven.[5]

Bullinger expresses no interest, however, in the questions he deems mere curiosities concerning God's part in Adam's sin. Indeed, God is not at all to be blamed for Adam's fall. He did not cause it and he certainly does not cause sin in the descendants of Adam. He remarks:

> Other questions, as whether God would have Adam fall, or whether he forced him to fall, or why he did not hinder his fall, and such like, we account among curious questions (unless perchance the frowardness[6] of heretics, or of men otherwise importunate, do compel us to open these points also out of the Word of God, as the godly doctors of the Church have oftentimes done); knowing that the Lord did forbid that man should eat of the forbidden fruit, and punished his transgression; and also that the things done are not evil in respect of the providence,

---

5. Schaff, *Creeds,* 3:843.

6. An archaic term meaning disposed to disobedience and opposition.

> will, and power of God, but in respect of Satan,
> and our will resisting the will of God.[7]

Bullinger's adoption of Augustine's doctrine of original sin, then, may make sense for his time, but since that day many have come to a different understanding of how sin works and how people become "infected" with it. It is rebellion. Rebellion is the act of the rebel and is not an inherited disposition. We are sinners, not because we are born sinners but because we choose to sin. In this respect, Bullinger's theology sounds very foreign to some modern Christians. Indeed, it is at this precise point of Bullinger's view of original sin that he is most estranged from modern Christianity.

And yet, Bullinger also recognizes the importance of human choice in the matter of sin. He writes:

> Let us now hear the other testimony concerning the corrupt will of man, which is in very deed the cause of sin. St James the apostle saith: "Let no man say when he is tempted, I am tempted of God: for God cannot be tempted with evil, neither tempteth he any man. But every man is tempted, when he is drawn away and enticed of his own concupiscence. Then when lust hath conceived, it bringeth forth sin; and sin, when it is finished, bringeth forth death." In these words St James, I hope, doth evidently enough make God to be free from all fault of sin, and doth derive it of us ourselves, shewing by the way the beginning and proceeding of sin.[8]

In Bullinger, then, we have a theologian with a foot in the world of Augustine (teaching that original sin is inherited sinfulness) and a foot in the world of modern theology

7. Schaff, *Creeds*, 3:844.
8. Bullinger, *Decades*, 3:372.

(attributing sin to our choice as the place where sin is born and from which it precedes). In Bullinger, then, sin is a self-imposed curse that has both genetic and intrinsic aspects. Sin ruins lives and brings everlasting death. And as a consequence of his love for fallen creatures, God intervenes to solve the problem caused by sin. To do so, God gives the law, whose power it to show humanity its powerlessness to achieve righteousness, and salvation through Christ, which alone brings real and meaningful justification. It is to Bullinger's understanding of the law that we now turn our attention.

THE LAW'S POWERLESSNESS TO SAVE

Put as simply as possible, the law given to Moses and communicated to Israel by its priests and prophets and enforced, at times, by its fairly small number of faithful kings cannot deliver ultimate deliverance from sin or its penalty. Sacrifices must be perpetually offered, year after year, for sin after sin. And even then redemption is never acquired, it is merely sought. Further, the powerlessness of the law to change hearts and minds was soon self-evident. What the law could do, and did end up doing, was make people aware that more was needed than the law if righteousness were to be a reality in the lives of the people of God. The law, in other words, for Bullinger, became and functioned as a marker of inadequacy and human need for a superhuman mediator.

Bullinger covered the law, and more particularly the Ten Commandments as the embodiment of the law, in the Second and Third *Decades*. To be more precise, the Second Decade, sermons 1 through 10, covers the law in general and the first through seventh Commandments, and the

Third Decade, sermons 1 through 4, finish off his discussion of the Commandments.

As he commences his sermon series on the law, Bullinger tells his audience that:

> THE law of God, openly published and proclaimed by the Lord our God himself, setteth down ordinary rules for us to know what we have to do, and what to leave undone, requiring obedience, and threatening utter destruction to disobedient rebels. This law is divided into the moral, ceremonial, and judicial laws: all which parts, and every point whereof, Moses hath very exquisitely written, and diligently expounded.[9]

Bullinger's distinction between the moral laws and the ceremonial laws is akin to the other Reformers' views on the issue of the law. The ceremonial laws, he believed, had to do with the Jews and the Jews alone and did not apply to Christians. The moral laws, on the other hand, did have to do with Christians and Christians were expected to abide by them. Christians and Jews are held accountable on the basis of their adherence to the law, and if they fall short of the laws demands, they are damned.

Furthermore, since no one actually keeps the law fully, all are damned. As Paul has it, "the wages of sin is death," following up on the Old Testament's "there is none righteous, no, not one" (Pss 14:3; 53:3). This is the one thing the law, then, does achieve: i.e., it makes people fully and absolutely aware of their own damnation. Here too Bullinger follows Paul.

After his very lengthy (if not more fairly described as long-winded) exposition of the various Commandments, Bullinger writes:

9. Bullinger, *Decades*, 2:209.

> The use of God's law is manifold and of sundry sorts; ... For first of all, the chief and proper office of the law is, to convince all men to be guilty of sin, and by their own fault to be the children of death.[10]

And then further on he adds:

> The second use and another office of the law is, to teach them that are justified in faith by Christ what to follow and what to eschew, and how the godly and faithful sort should worship.[11]

The law, then, not only convinces people of their own sinfulness; it also serves to guide believers into the sorts of behaviors that are proper to the Christian. The law guides. First, it guides to an awareness of damnation, and then it guides to behavior suitable for those redeemed.

Finally Bullinger sees a third purpose of the law, which he describes as follows:

> The third use or office of the law is to repress the unruly; and those whom no reason can move to orderliness the law commandeth to constrain with punishment, that honesty, peace, and public tranquillity, may be maintained in christian commonweals.[12]

In sum, Bullinger's view on the law is that the law informs us of our damnation, guides us to morality and righteousness, and excoriates the unruly among us.

But of course if God were simply to give us the law, fully aware that we could not adhere to it and that our damnation was certain because of it, he would be quite

---

10. Bullinger, *Decades*, 3:237.
11. Bullinger, *Decades*, 3:243.
12. Bullinger, *Decades*, 3:244–45.

cruel and mischievous. But God is not cruel or mischievous and accordingly he provides for our salvation by another means: the sacrifice of Christ, on our behalf, who dies for our sins. And doing so, justifies us. It is to the understanding Bullinger has towards the doctrine of justification that we now turn our attention.

JUSTIFICATION

In his little book titled "The Grace of God" Bullinger offers this declaration of justification: "Justification comes . . . only from the sheer grace, love, faithfulness, and promise of God." This does not mean, of course, that once justified we need do nothing. On the contrary, justification, the act by which we are declared innocent of our sins and right with God, makes it possible for us to do things that do please God.

Bullinger, as we by now have come to expect, goes into the greatest detail about the justification of the believer through faith in Christ in his lengthy sixth sermon of the first *Decade*. First, of course, it is necessary to define exactly what justification is:

> To justify is as much to say as to quit from judgment and from the denounced and uttered sentence of condemnation. It signifieth to remit offences, to cleanse, to sanctify, and to give inheritance of life everlasting.[13]

Bullinger believed, and he does so along with the bulk of Christian theologians up to that moment in the history of Christianity, that justification is the act by which we are made to be right with God, in spite of our sins, because those sins have been forgiven as a result of the sacrifice of

13. Bullinger, *Decades*, 1:105.

Christ on behalf of humanity. Or, in Bullinger's own words (which are many, but which must be shared in full in order to demonstrate his thought clearly):

> Imagine therefore, that man is set before the judgment-seat of God, and that there he is pleaded guilty; to wit, that he is accused and convinced of heinous offences, and therefore sued to punishment or to the sentence of condemnation. Imagine also, that the Son of God maketh intercession, and cometh in as a mean, desiring that upon him may be laid the whole fault and punishment due unto us men, that he by his death may cleanse them and take them away, setting us free from death, and giving us life everlasting. Imagine too, that God, the most high and just judge, receiveth the offer, and translateth the punishment together with the fault from us unto the neck of his Son; making therewithal a statute, that whosoever believeth that the Son of God suffered for the sins of the world, brake the power of death, and delivered us from damnation, should be cleansed from his sins and made heir of life everlasting.[14]

Few theologians have managed to say it as clearly or, frankly, as concisely as Bullinger here manages to do.

What he does next, though, in his treatment of the topic, is not frequently done by the theologians who preceded him. To be sure, Reformed theology has followed his procedure quite closely. But in Bullinger's era, the next step was quite bold, because next Bullinger asserts that faith, without the benefit of works at all, alone justifies.

The history of the doctrine of justification by faith alone, most famously associated with Luther and Zwingli and Calvin, is one of the most fascinating in all historical

14. Bullinger, *Decades*, 1:105.

theology. Naturally we cannot enter into such a discussion here. Suffice it to say, those interested in the doctrine of justification ought to read further on the subject. An excellent starting point is Alister McGrath's *Iustitia Dei: A History of the Christian Doctrine of Justification*, the fourth edition of which was published in 2020 by Cambridge University Press.

Returning to Bullinger, as he proceeds through the sermon in which he instructs his congregation about this critical doctrine, he marshals scriptural evidence time and again. Sensitive to the context of each passage he cites, and citing the texts he uses in their proper contexts (because Bullinger was an excellent exegete who understood the utter importance of context for interpretation), Bullinger bolsters and advances his case. Primarily drawing from Romans and Galatians, Bullinger teaches justification.

Importantly, having shown that we are justified strictly by faith, good works will nonetheless follow. Justification takes place first. But if good works do not follow, there has been no reception of the justifying act. Bullinger says it quite beautifully in fact, writing:

> True faith is the well-spring and root of all virtues and good works: and first of all, it satisfieth the mind and desire of man, and maketh it quiet and joyful. For the Lord in the gospel saith: "I am the bread of life: he that cometh to me shall not hunger; and he that believeth in me shall not thirst at any time." For what can he desire more, which doth already feel, that by true faith he possesseth the very Son of God, in whom are all the heavenly treasures, and in whom is all fulness and grace?[15]

---

15. Bullinger, *Decades*, 1:120.

Justification changes its recipients from the inside out, utterly.

What is often overlooked in the debate about justification by faith versus justification by works is the fact that the very act of justification itself is life-changing. It's a new birth. Bullinger not only understands that, he expounds it.

> For when we affirm that we are justified by faith, or when we make faith the cause of justification, (which thing must be by often repetition beaten into our memories,) we do not understand that faith, as it is a virtue in us, doth work, and by the quality that sticketh to us doth merit, righteousness in the sight of God; but so often as we make mention of faith, we understand the grace of God exhibited in Christ, which is through faith freely applied to us, and received as the free gift of God bestowed upon us.[16]

This "free gift of God" is given to us and when apprehended, results in a life that is devoted to God and lived by the power of the fruits of the Spirit (Gal 5:22), which are love, joy, peace, patience, kindness, gentleness, meekness, and self control. In Bullinger's beautiful phrasing:

> These I say and all other virtues the Holy Ghost, which worketh all good things in all men, graffeth, planteth, preserveth, defendeth, and bringeth unto full ripeness in the minds of the faithful.[17]

This is not the place to delve further into the ministry of the Spirit in the life of the believer. That subject has been discussed above. It is the place, however, to summarize Bullinger's teaching on sin and redemption.

16. Bullinger, *Decades*, 3:334.
17. Bullinger, *Decades*, 4:322.

Sin affects, infects, and defects everything that it touches and it touches human beings completely. God, in response to this self-imposed self-destruction by his children, sends his Son to take the place of fallen humans on the cross and there he dies because of their sins. But of course the death of Christ is not the end of the story. He rises from the dead, and ascends into heaven, from whence he shall return to claim his own for eternity.

Sin, in the theology of Bullinger, does not have the last word. Salvation does.

QUESTIONS FOR DISCUSSION

1. What is the meaning of sin for Bullinger?
2. What is the nature of salvation according to Bullinger?
3. What do you see as the main strengths and weaknesses of Bullinger's teaching on salvation?

8

CHURCH AND MINISTRY

HEINRICH BULLINGER HAD A robust doctrine of the church and its ministry. Predestination and salvation led to Christians being called together into the one "body of Christ" (1 Cor 12:27; Eph 4:12). Salvation necessarily involves community—the communion of the "saints" of God (1 Cor 1:2) with the God who elected and called them; and Christian believers with one another in the "household of God" (Eph 2:19). There is no "solitary Christianity" in Bullinger's view. The church is not an "option" in the Christian life. It is an absolute necessity. The church is God's way of work and witness in this world. The head of the church is Jesus Christ. The message of the church is that "Jesus is Lord" (Rom 10:9), the "savior of the world" (1 John 4:14).

The church exists because of the goodness of God. Bullinger said that "so great is the goodness of our good God" that God does not want to "live happily and blessedly alone." God wants to pour out on God's human creatures "all kind of blessedness; and . . . we should enjoy his goods by all means possible." So God chooses a people to be God's own people who live in this world and with whom God "may dwell." God enriches them with "goods" and in their lives—God reigns! They are called by God's name and are "a people, a house, a kingdom, an inheritance, a flock, a congregation or church, of the living God."[1]

Relatedly, "because God from the beginning would have men to be saved, and to come to the knowledge of the truth (1 Tim 2:4), it is altogether necessary that there always should have been, and should be now, and to the end of the world a Church."[2] The church is the means by which salvation, the knowledge of truth—in Jesus Christ, is made known and received in the world. So the church is always necessary and crucial.

Bullinger offers an elaborate definition of the church in his Second Helvetic Confession:

> The Church is an assembly of the faithful called or gathered out of the world; a communion, I say, of all saints, namely, of those who truly know and rightly worship and serve the true God in Christ the Savior, by the Word and Holy Spirit, and who by faith are partakers of all benefits which are freely offered through Christ.[3]

God calls the church into being as those who know, worship, and serve God in Christ. The church lives by the Word and the Holy Spirit. It is marked by faith, which brings the benefits of God in Christ. More compactly, Bullinger said the church is "the company, communion, congregation, multitude, or fellowship of all that profess the name

---

1. Bullinger, *Decades*, 5:41.
2. Cochrane, ed., *Reformed Confessions*, 261.
3. Cochrane, ed., *Reformed Confessions*, 261.

of Christ."[4] The church and its members are united in its common confession of the name of Christ.

Bullinger believed that this common confession of Christ is expressed in the church's life and practices. A common commitment to "true doctrine" and the use of the sacraments conveys the church's unity:

> The church is the whole company and multitude of the faithful, partly being now in heaven, and partly remaining yet here upon earth: where it doth agree plainly in unity of faith or true doctrine, and in the lawful partaking of the sacraments; neither is it divided, but joined and united together as it were in one house and fellowship.[5]

Common unity in Christ is a feature of the church which is spread throughout the world. This is the meaning confessed in the Apostles' Creed: I believe in "the holy catholic church." "Catholic" means universal. So Bullinger said: "We, therefore, call this Church catholic because it is universal, scattered through all parts of the world, and extended unto all times, and is not limited to any times or places."[6] Bullinger was thus critical of heretical sects like the Donatists in the early church who confined the "true church" only to the areas they inhabited, as Bullinger said, "to I know not what corners of Africa." "Nor," he continued, "do we approve of the Roman clergy who have recently passed off only the Roman Church as catholic."[7] Bullinger commented that

---

4. Bullinger, *Decades*, 1:161.
5. Bullinger, *Decades*, 5:5.
6. Cochrane, ed., *Reformed Confessions*, 262.
7. Cochrane, ed., *Reformed Confessions*, 262.

> the church of God is not tied to any one region, nation, or kindred; to condition, age, sex or kind: all the faithful generally and each one specially, wherever they or he be, are citizens and members of this church. St Paul the Apostle saith: "There is neither Jew nor Greek, neither bond man nor free, neither man or woman; for ye be all one in Christ Jesu" [Gal 3:28].[8]

Comprehensively, the universal church "stretcheth out itself through the compass of the world, and unto all ages, and doth contain all the faithful from the first Adam even unto the very last saint that shall be remaining before the end of the world."[9] Yet, the universal church has particular expressions—a "communion of saints" in localized times and places—throughout history and throughout the world. All these are united together in their bond of faith with Jesus Christ, no matter where they are or when they have existed.

Like other Protestants, Bullinger distinguished two types of the church: The church "triumphant" and the church "militant." He wrote that

> the triumphant is that great company of holy spirits in heaven, triumphing for the victory gotten against the world, sin, and the devil, still enjoying the sight of God, wherein consisteth all fulness of all kind of joy and pleasure: whereupon they set forth God's glory, and praise his goodness for ever. (Rev. 7).[10]

The church triumphant is the church of God's elect, now unhindered by sin, and living eternally in glory in the worship and praise of God.

8. Bullinger, *Decades*, 5:5.
9. Bullinger, *Decades*, 1:161.
10. Bullinger, *Decades*, 5:5.

Church and Ministry

The church "militant" is "a congregation . . . upon earth, professing the name and religion of Christ, continually fighting in the world against the devil, sin, flesh, and the world, in the camp and tents and under the banner of our Lord Christ."[11] The church on earth, now, is the "visible" church in the sense that it consists of those who profess faith in Christ and participate in the worship and life of the church. The genuineness of their professions of faith cannot be judged by humans, only by God. So, the "church militant" is visible; but whether members of this visible church will ultimately be part of the church triumphant, after death, is left to the judgment of God.[12]

The church militant is "marked by God with certain tokens and marks whereby it may be known in this world." These are "two special and principal marks," which are "the sincere preaching of the word of God, and the lawful partaking of the sacraments of Christ."[13] These two "marks" were distinctive for Protestants and became primary focuses to describe the nature of the church and its ministries.[14] Jesus Christ gave himself for the church "to make her holy by cleansing her with the washing of water by the word" (Eph 5:26). God, in grace, gives ways or marks by which this message of Christ can be known here and now in the church. Said Bullinger, God's Word is "to be received by faith, and sealeth with sacraments, that the faithful should

---

11. Bullinger, *Decades*, 5:7.

12. Another, similar distinction is between the "visible church," which is the outward, organized church on earth, and the "invisible church"—seen only by the eyes of God: which is the genuine believers in Christ on earth and in heaven (the elect). Bullinger calls these the "outward" (visible) and "inward" (invisible) church: "Of God's church there was one visible and outward and another invisible and inward," See *Decades*, 5:17.

13. Bullinger, *Decades*, 5:17.

14. See below on "Word and Sacraments" in chapter 9.

doubt of nothing touching their salvation obtained through Christ." God not only provides salvation in Jesus Christ, but calls the church together and provides ways by which believers can have firm belief in their salvation in Christ. This is God's gracious provision of the church!

Word and sacraments as marks of the church are efficacious or effective only by faith for those who belong to God's covenant family. As Bullinger put it: "All these testimonies properly (as I said a little before) do belong unto the elect members of God, being endued with faith and true obedience: but unto the hypocrites, which are void of faith and due obedience, they nothing at all belong."[15] Faith in Jesus Christ is the key ingredient through which the preaching of the Word and the sacraments of the church becomes means of salvation and the ongoing life of obedience to God in Christ.

While the church triumphant and the "invisible" church are composed of God's elect, the church militant (and the "visible" church) is a "mixed body" (Lat. *corpus permixtum*, as St. Augustine said). Biblical parables point this out: the parable of the wheat (Matt 13:24–30) and the parable of the good fish and bad fish (Matt 13:47–50). It is not a human task to judge the genuineness of anyone's faith. It is God who knows the heart (1 Sam 16:7). The "outward marks" of preaching and the sacraments are shared by those who have genuine faith and those who don't, in the visible church.

But Bullinger went on to say:

> Beside those outward marks of the church which the true believers have common with hypocrites, there are certain inward marks specially belonging only to the godly; or else, if you will, rather call them bonds or proper gifts. These do make

15. Bullinger, *Decades*, 5:19.

> the outward marks to be fruitful, and, without the outward marks being by some necessity absent, do make men worthy or acceptable in the sight of God. For without these no man can please God: in these therefore is the true mark of God's children.[16]

The "inward marks" of which Bullinger spoke are "the fellowship of God's Spirit, a sincere faith, and double charity: for by these the faithful, being the true and lively members of Christ, are united and knit together, first unto their head Christ, then to all the members of the ecclesiastical body."[17] These are the genuine realities of faith—living in communion or fellowship with the Spirit of God who leads and guides the church and Christian believers; the sincere faith which is focused on Christ's loving redemption in salvation; and "double charity": loving God and loving neighbor as God's law commands (Deut 6:5; Lev 19:18) and Jesus reinforced (Mark 12:30–32). These inward marks of true faith unite the church with it head, Jesus Christ; and unite all members of the church with each other in the body of Christ.

Can the church err? Does the presence of "hypocrites" in the visible church (church militant) mean the church can be led away from God's truth? The church triumphant (in heaven) "can never err."[18] It is composed of God's elect in the eternal presence of the living God. But for the church on earth, the danger of falling into error is real. When those who participate in the "outward marks" of the church do not also participate in the "inward marks" of the church, then drifts into errors of doctrine or practice can happen.

Bullinger honestly acknowledges this situation:

16. Bullinger, *Decades*, 5:23.
17. Bullinger, *Decades*, 5:23.
18. Bullinger, *Decades*, 5:35.

> If we understand the wicked or hypocrites joined and mingled with the good, and the wicked alone by themselves, they do nothing else but err; but as they are joined unto the good and faithful, and follow them, they either err, or they err not. For the church of the good and faithful here upon earth doth err, and doth not err.[19]

It is imperative for the church militant to hold fast to God's Word, trust in God's grace, and for the church to pray for the forgiveness of sins: "For always, so long as it is living here on earth, it prayeth heartily: 'And forgive us our trespasses.'"[20] In *state*, Bullinger wrote that the church "does not err as long as it rests upon the rock Christ, and upon the foundation of the prophets and apostles."[21] So the church militant lives by faith and the forgiveness of God's grace.

There is no "perfect church" here and now. The church which is "holy and without blemish" (Eph 5:27) can be said to be so, said Bullinger, only

> through the benefit of Christ's sanctification; not that by herself, while she is in the flesh, she is without spot; but for that those spots, indeed otherwise cleaving unto her, through the innocency of Christ, to those that embrace Christ by faith are not imputed: finally, for that the selfsame church in the world to come shall be without spot or wrinkle.

When the Apostles' Creed speaks of the "holy" catholic church, the church's "holiness" now can only be by Christ's work of preserving the church and Christ's holiness and

---

19. Bullinger, *Decades*, 5:35.

20. Bullinger, *Decades*, 5:35–36.

21. Cochrane, ed., *Reformed Confessions*, 263. This is because the church errs "in doctrine and faith, as often as she, turning from Christ and his word" *Decades,* 5:37.

"innocency," which is given to the church. Christ takes on the church's sin and the sins of believers in the church who embrace Christ by faith. In and because of Christ, sin is forgiven. Thus, Bullinger said, "Chiefly by the benefit of imputation, the church erreth not, but is most pure and without sin."[22]

This dependency on Jesus Christ comes as the church gains its life and lives in dependence on "the grace of our Lord Jesus Christ" (1 Thess 5:28) who is the head of the church (Col 1:18). Bullinger spoke very harshly of the Roman Catholic Church, whose bishops he accused of "tyranny over the church," even of "playing the part of very antichrists in the temple of God."[23] Thus, Bullinger and others became "true members of Christ and of his saints, flying out of the popish church" and are "gathered together again into one holy catholic and apostolic church. And this church we do acknowledge to be the very house of God, and the proper sheepfold of Christ our Lord, whereof he is the shepherd."[24] For the church "is the house of God, the chief master-builder thereof being God himself."[25] Indeed, "The true master-builder of this house of God saith in the gospel: 'Upon this rock I will build my church.' (Matt, xvi.) For the same Son of God is he that maketh us worthy of his kingdom; he giveth us faith, by which we are made true members of the church of God."[26] It is Peter's confession: "You are the Messiah, the Son of the living God" that led Jesus to respond: "And I tell you, you are Peter, and on this rock I will build my church, and the gates of Hades will

---

22. See Bullinger, *Decades*, 5:36 for these citations.
23. Bullinger, *Decades*, 5:64.
24. Bullinger, *Decades*, 5:65.
25. Bullinger, *Decades*, 5:79.
26. Bullinger, *Decades*, 5:79.

not prevail against it" (Matt 16:16, 18).[27] The church is grounded in its head, Jesus Christ as God's Messiah, bringing salvation to the world.

Salvation comes to the world in Jesus Christ, who is himself God's kingdom,[28] and is thus the Lord of the church. Said Bullinger: "Moreover, this church of the faithful is called the kingdom of God: for the Son of God himself, Christ Jesus, is the king of the church, that is to say, of all the faithful; who by his Spirit and word governeth the church; and she again willingly submitteth herself to his government."[29] All members of Christ's church are "united to their head Christ by faith; the head itself is joined to the members through grace and the Spirit. Christ is never separated from the church: neither hath she life elsewhere but from Christ; who although he be absent in body from the militant church, yet is he continually present in spirit, in operation, and in government."[30] The great head of the church is always with the church by the Spirit and at work in the church by the same Spirit. For "Christ is the head, for he ruleth all things in heaven and in earth; he governeth all things; he hath all things subject unto himself; and maketh

27. Bullinger, *Decades*, 5:81. Bullinger wrote: "Christ said not, I will build my church (Matt. xvi.) upon thee, but upon a rock; and that self-same rock that thou hast confessed." This was a bedrock Protestant contention—against reading this text as a justification of the papacy, as did Roman Catholics.

28. For Bullinger, Jesus is the locus of the kingdom or the place where the kingdom is found; just as Jesus Christ is the substance of the covenant (see ch. 6, n. 26). In this description of the kingdom, Bullinger hearkens back to early church theologians, such as Origen, who said the kingdom is (Gk.) *autobaselia*—a "self-kingdom"—the kingdom is Jesus Christ himself.

29. Bullinger, *Decades*, 5:84. Bullinger wrote that the church cannot "be governed by any other spirit than by the Spirit of Christ," Cochrane, ed., *Reformed Confessions*, 263.

30. Bullinger, *Decades*, 5:85.

the church his body, ministering unto her those things whereof she hath need, and fulfilling all her desires" (Eph 5). The church is indissolubly united (by faith) with Jesus Christ, as a vine and its branches (John 15:5). Jesus makes the church his body and ministers to the church, always. As Bullinger said, "Christ our Lord is the universal pastor, and chief and Lord of pastors."[31]

MINISTRY

The ministry of the church is centered in Jesus Christ as ministers in the church proclaim the Word of God and administer the sacraments. Pastors convey Jesus Christ, the Lord of the church, in exercising their ministries in accord with the call of God and the call of the church.

God has chosen to use ministers to build up the church. Bullinger notes:

> God has always used ministers for the gathering or establishing of a Church for himself, and for the governing and preservation of the same; and still he does, and always will, use them so long as the Church remains on earth. Therefore, the first beginning, institution, and office of ministers is a most ancient arrangement of God himself, and not a new one of men.[32]

This is God's decision and, Bullinger said, it was because of God's "exceeding goodness and wherefore mercy toward us," that God "coveteth to pour himself wholly into us."[33]

God could have carried out the ministry of the church another way. For "it is true that God can, by his power,

---

31. Bullinger, *Decades*, 5:86.
32. Cochrane, ed., *Reformed Confessions*, 268.
33. Bullinger, *Decades*, 5:93.

without any means join to himself a Church from among men; but he preferred to deal with men by the ministry of men." This is another example of God's "accommodation" in adapting God's purposes to the capacities of humans. Since God uses humans to carry out the divine work, "therefore ministers are to be regarded, not as ministers by themselves alone, but as the ministers of God, inasmuch as God effects the salvation of men through them," said Bullinger.[34] The divine character of the ministry comes from God's work in using ministers to bring salvation to others. More fully, wrote Bullinger:

> when ministers bear witness of the Son of God, and out of his word promise life everlasting, their word is not called man's word, but the word of God; and they are said to save, and to release from sin; for they are the true messengers and heralds of the King, who is the deliverer, who hath sent them to publish remission of sins: whereupon also they attribute all the means of life, salvation, and delivery, to the only deliverer Christ.[35]

Ministers are the means God uses to bring the message of salvation as the Word of God to sinners. The savior is Christ; the minister is a person whom God has called to this work.

The ministry is not to be despised—by saying salvation is by the Holy Spirit "in such a way that we make void the ecclesiastical ministry." Several Scriptures are cited to indicate the need for preaching to carry out the application of salvation (Rom 10:14, 17; John 13:20; Acts 16:9; and 1 Cor 3:9).[36]

34. Cochrane, ed., *Reformed Confessions*, 268.
35. Bullinger, *Decades*, 5:97–98.
36. Cochrane, ed., *Reformed Confessions*, 268–69.

"On the other hand," wrote Bullinger, "we must beware that we do not attribute too much to ministers and the ministry"—citing John 6:44 and 1 Cor 3:5ff.—to indicate the work of salvation and growth in faith is the work of God and not a human work by a minister. "Therefore," we should recognize God moves the hearts of persons: "Let us believe that God teaches us by his word, outwardly through his ministers, and inwardly moves the hearts of his elect to faith by the Holy Spirit; and that therefore we ought to render all glory unto God for this whole favor."[37] An "outward/inward" pattern is applicable here in ascribing the initiation and action of salvation to God who uses human ministers as the means or instruments by which salvation is proclaimed. This means too that "the minister doth not take on him the honour of God and the work of the Spirit, but his own work, that is to say, the ministry."[38]

Bullinger's repeated emphasis—throughout his whole theology—on the work of God as the initiation and source of things that matter most is found in other teachings about the ministers and the work of ministry. For example, Bullinger notes how God has used persons to do God's work of teaching about God: the patriarchs, Moses, prophets, and teachers, and then God "even sent his only-begotten Son, the most perfect teacher of the world; in whom is hidden the wisdom of God, and which has come to us through the most holy, simple, and most perfect doctrine of all." Even Jesus used others to carry out his ongoing work.

> [Jesus] chose disciples for himself whom he made apostles. These went out into the whole world, and everywhere gathered together churches by the preaching of the Gospel, and

37. Cochrane, ed., *Reformed Confessions*, 269. Cf. Bullinger, *Decades*, 5:94.

38. Bullinger, *Decades*, 5:100.

> then throughout all the churches in the world they appointed pastors or teachers, according to Christ's command; through their successors he has taught and governed the Church until this day.[39]

God's "choosing" of those who serve as ministers shows God's work not only in salvation but also in calling and appointing persons to specific ministries of service. These are examples of prominent persons; but God works within the body of the church itself to appoint persons to ministries that serve the gospel.

In the leadership of the church, to this day, God has appointed people to various ministries. "The ministers of the new people are called by various names," wrote Bullinger. "For they are called apostles, prophets, evangelists, bishops, elders, pastors, and teachers (1 Cor. 12:28; Eph. 4:11)."[40] Each of these ministries in the church has its own function to carry out.

In Bullinger's early ministry, he stressed the "prophetic office" of those who interpreted Scripture and proclaimed the Word of God as preachers.[41] In his later period, Bullinger distinguished between those had the particular calling of a prophet and those who performed the daily ministries of the church, as pastors. Bullinger continued to teach that "prophets" are "also found still today."[42]

Evangelists were "heralds of the Gospel of Christ" and Timothy was urged to "do the work of an evangelist" (2 Tim 4:5). Bishops oversee and keep watch over the church, administering food and tending to the "needs of the life of the Church." Presbyters are "elders" who govern the church

39. Cochrane, ed., *Reformed Confessions*, 269.
40. Cochrane, ed., *Reformed Confessions*, 270.
41. On this, see Daniel Bolliger, in *Architect*, 173.
42. Cochrane, ed., *Reformed Confessions*, 270.

with "wholesome counsel." Pastors "keep the Lord's sheepfold, and also provide for its needs." Teachers "instruct and teach the true faith and godliness." This means, said Bullinger, that "the ministers of the churches may now be called bishops, elders, pastors, and teachers."[43] Bullinger contrasted this basic ministerial structure for the church—as drawn from Scripture and apostolic practice with the elaborate ministerial structure of the Roman Catholic Church where many functions are given, including acolytes, exorcist, cantors, porters, etc. "For us," Bullinger said, "the apostolic doctrine concerning ministers is enough."[44]

In these offices of ministry, Bullinger was committed to the theological conviction that God chose ministry to be carried out in the church by those appointed by the church and that these persons are working in cooperation with God and with each other. God uses persons to carry out God's ministries. As Paul said to the Corinthian church: "We are God's servants, working together; you are God's field, God's building" (1 Cor 3:9). This is so the gospel can be proclaimed and the message of salvation given to the world. It is not the talents or abilities of individual persons that are highlighted for preaching and ministry. It is rather

---

43. Cochrane, ed., *Reformed Confessions*, 270. In his *Decades*, Bullinger mentioned the biblical "deacons" as participants of ministry in the early church. Bullinger believed "the office of deacons was separated from the function of pastors; and therefore we do not reckon them in the order of pastors. The ancient fathers referred them to the ministry, but not to the priesthood." Deacons included women who served; 5:107. To "these elders and deacons were helpers: the deacons in seeing to the poor; and the elders in doctrine, in discipline, and in governing and sustaining other weightier affairs of the church," 5:108–9. So Bullinger recognized the work of deacons, especially in the care of the poor (as Calvin had done in Geneva). But he did not consider their helping ministries as "offices" in the church in the same way other offices were given to the church.

44. Cochrane, ed., *Reformed Confessions*, 270.

God's choosing to use those called to these ministries to cooperate with God's will and purposes. The work of the gospel is a common enterprise as an overall ministry of the church. Thus there must be cooperation. There needs also to be a kind of "functional equality" throughout the church's ministries.

The church ordains its ministers "by lawful and ecclesiastical election" in a "proper order without any uproar, dissention and rivalry."[45] Those called must have "the necessary gifts of a pastor." They serve in obedience to Jesus Christ; and "one and an equal power or function is given to all ministers in the Church." For, as Bullinger reminded, Jesus said, "Let the leader among you become as one who serves" (Luke 22:26). Ministers have "kept themselves in humility, and by mutual services they helped one another in the governing and preserving of the Church."[46]

The duties of ministers, said Bullinger, "are various; yet for the most part they are restricted to two, in which all the rest are comprehended: to the teaching of the Gospel of Christ, and to the proper administration of the sacraments."[47] Those who "expound God's Word" are "to apply the whole doctrine to the care and use of the Church." Preaching has a focus and a function. This is so "that what

---

45. Cochrane, ed., *Reformed Confessions*, 271. Concern for the order of the church means the church is "not to look for a secret inspiration with the heretics Enthusiastae; but to acknowledge a just order, and that God himself speaketh unto us by men, of whom he would have us to learn religion," *Decades* 5:94. In this and other matters of ministry, Bullinger wrote against views of Anabaptists and their views the ministers should be simple (Matt 11:25) and not learned.

46. Cochrane, ed., *Reformed Confessions*, 274. Stephens writes of Bullinger that "ministers are reminded that 'they are ministers, not masters of the churches.' Further they are 'not ministers or authors of faith, but instruments through whom God acts.'" Cf, Stephens, *Theology*, 337.

47. Cochrane, ed., *Reformed Confessions*, 275.

is taught may benefit the hearers and edify the faithful." Teaching for learning and understanding is key; and teaching in such a way that those who hear may be built up and strengthened in their faith and devotion to God in Christ (edification; cf. Rom 15:2; 2 Cor 10:8). Ministers are to teach and exhort, to comfort and strengthen "the fainthearted," to rebuke, convince, and "raise the fallen." In administering the sacraments, ministers are to "preserve the faithful in a holy unity," catechize, "commend the needs of the poor to the Church," to "visit, instruct, and keep in the way of life the sick and those afflicted with various temptations," to "attend to public prayers or supplications in times of need," and "to see to everything that pertains to the tranquility, peace and welfare of the churches."[48]

Discipline, is also part of the church's life—"an absolute necessity in the Church" and it "falls to ministers," said Bullinger, "to regulate this discipline for edification, according to the circumstances of the time, public state, and necessity." Through it all, "at all times and in all places the rule is to be observed that everything is to be done for edification, decently and honorably, without oppression and strife."[49]

God's purpose in the church and the establishment of ministries within the church is theological. Bullinger wrote: "All the members of the ecclesiastical body are wonderfully glued together by the ecclesiastical ministry: for this chiefly helpeth to make concord and continue unity."[50]

God's work in church and ministry is of crucial significance. It is the way the predestination of God and the salvation of God's people are enacted and carried out in this world. Bullinger put it clearly:

48. Cochrane, ed., *Reformed Confes*sions, 275.
49. Cochrane, ed., *Reformed Confes*sions, 276.
50. Bullinger, *Decades*, 5:100–101.

> God hath instituted a ministry in the church, that all the members may be brought into the unity of the body, and that they may be subject and cleave to Christ their head, that thereby we may grow.... Being joined together in true faith and charity, let us hold fast the pure and simple truth of Christ; and serving Christ unfeignedly in this world, we may after death reign with him in heaven.[51]

QUESTIONS FOR DISCUSSION

1. In what ways is the "church" a key and important part of Bullinger's theology?
2. What are the similarities and differences between the "church militant" and the "church triumphant" in Bullinger's view?
3. In what ways is the ministry of the church an example of God's "accommodation" in relating to humanity?
4. Why is it important for the church to have an ordered or structured ministry?

---

51. Bullinger, *Decades*, 5:101.

9

WORD AND SACRAMENTS

HEINRICH BULLINGER FIRMLY BELIEVED that the church was most present in the world in the twofold act of the preaching of the Word and the administration of the sacraments.[1] Bullinger's clearest exposition of the power of the Word and the sacraments to effect change in the lives of Christians is found in his little volume from 1555 titled "The Salvation of Believers."

Naturally, though, we learn a great deal about Bullinger's understanding of both the preaching of the Word and the administration of the sacraments in his sermons, the *Decades*.

THE PREACHER AND THE PREACHING OF THE WORD

Of primary importance, for Bullinger, is the person and work of the pastor. The pastor is the administrator of the

1. Key to any further reading on the topic of this chapter is Stephens' *Theology*, 345–71.

sacraments and the pastor is the proclaimer of the Word. He writes:

> I say there shall be needful of a strait trial of life and perfect examination of learning: for this is not a matter of small weight; the whole safety of the church hangeth hereupon. If any unworthy and unlearned be ordained, the whole church for the most part is neglected, led astray, and overthrown. But we do not mean a childlike and scholar like examination; but a grave and strait examination of knowledge in the scripture and the true interpretation thereof, of the charge of a pastor, of the mysteries of sound faith, and of other such like points.[2]

Bullinger is not exaggerating when he maintains that the health and wellbeing of the church hangs on the reality of its having educationally qualified and doctrinally competent pastors. Few places where the Reformation reached were as "pro-educated-clergy" as Zurich. It was under the leadership of Zwingli himself years earlier that Zurich had established the "Prophezei." This was the forerunner of the University of Zurich and in it members of the clergy and interested lay people met each week day (except market day, Friday) early in the morning, year round, in the chapel of the Great Minster, to learn the content and meaning of Scripture. The text was read in Latin, and a Hebrew or Greek reading followed, depending on the passage. This was followed by Zwingli's own exposition. And then further explanations were provided by the various experts in Hebrew and Greek.

This important educational opportunity was offered and indeed attendance was required of all pastors in the region under Zurich's control.

2. Bullinger, *Decades*, 5:135.

When Bullinger took charge of the Zurich church, the idea that clergy should be highly educated was part of the very fabric of the Reformed Church of Zurich. Bullinger supplemented Zwingli's emphasis on knowledge of the Bible with a clearer focus for the pastor as interpreter and exegete, responsible only for the accurate promulgation of God's Word. He opines, rather lengthily, but importantly, that

> the chief office of a pastor of the church is, to use those very keys which the Lord hath delivered to his apostles, and no other; that is, to preach the only and pure word of God, and not to fetch any doctrine from any other place than out of the very word of God. For there is a perpetual and inviolable law at this day also laid upon our pastors, which we read was laid upon the most ancient governors of the church, the Lord himself witnessing in Malachi, and saying: "My covenant was with Levi of life and peace; and I gave him fear, and he feared me, and was afraid before my name. The law of truth was in his mouth, and there was no iniquity found in his lips; he walked with me in peace and equity, and turned many from their iniquity. For the priest's lips should preserve knowledge, and they should seek the law at his mouth: for he is the messenger of the Lord of hosts."[3]

Being the messenger of the Lord of Hosts was both the privilege and the terror of the pastoral office.

As Bullinger considers the pastoral office he wishes not only to stress its exegetical function but also its limitations and its methods. The ministry is not established for the aggrandizement of the preacher (as the Catholics exalt

---

3. Bullinger, *Decades*, 5:149–50.

their bishops and popes to near divine status). Instead, the imperfect person called to ministry remains imperfect and can only fulfill his office (in Bullinger's day only men could be called to be pastors) when aided by the Spirit of God. The minister must remain, nonetheless, a paragon of virtue and morality. This is the tightrope the pastor must walk: imperfect creature being morally and ethically upright. Bullinger writes, "Let the ministry indeed be beautified and kept in authority, but let it be done without the dishonouring of God."[4]

No pastor should dishonor God as he ministers. The consequences of this moral uprightness has extremely practical effects:

> And therefore when ministers bear witness of the Son of God, and out of his word promise life everlasting, their word is not called man's word, but the word of God; and they are said to save, and to release from sin; for they are the true messengers and heralds of the King, who is the deliverer, who hath sent them to publish remission of sins: whereupon also they attribute all the means of life, salvation, and delivery, to the only deliverer Christ.[5]

Given the seriousness of the work, only those are fit for it who are called by God himself. Bullinger was an inveterate foe of the Anabaptists for their acceptance of illegitimately appointed pastors. The claim of a man who one day stands behind a plow and the next day ascends into the pulpit merely because he had some sense of an "inner calling" without undergoing the requisite training and education was a disaster for the church. He expresses himself

---

4. Bullinger, *Decades*, 5:96.
5. Bullinger, *Decades*, 5:97–98.

quite clearly on the topic when, whilst discussing the various sorts of pastors and their callings, he remarks:

> The fourth kind of calling is that, whereby any man thrusteth himself into the ministry of his own private affection, being neither ordained of God, neither yet by man. Of these kind of men the Lord saith in Jeremiah: "I have not sent them, and yet they ran." Cyprian, writing unto Antonianus, calleth such schismatics, who usurp unto them the office of a bishop, no man giving it them. And this kind of calling is improperly called a calling.[6]

There is only one sort of pastor that is appropriate and that is the pastor properly called. Bullinger writes, in some detail:

> Wherefore it is evident, that in the church there must needs be a calling, and that public and lawful; as well for many other causes, as especially for these: that the ordinance of God be not neglected, and that the discipline of the church be retained, and that all men in the church may know who are preferred to the ecclesiastical ministry. Albeit therefore Paul, the apostle and doctor of the Gentiles, in the beginning were not sent of men, neither by men, but of God only; yet the same Paul, at the commandment of the Holy Ghost, is separated by the church of Antioch, together with Barnabas, to the ministry of the Gentiles. After the same manner many other were sent or called of God; whom nevertheless it behoved to be ordained also by men. For Paul in another place saith: "And no man taketh this honour unto himself, but he that is called of God, as was Aaron." And again: "How shall

6. Bullinger, *Decades*, 5:131.

> they hear without a preacher, and how shall they
> preach except they be sent?" &c.[7]

The preaching office, then, for Bullinger, is only properly occupied by those properly called and qualified. Only then and by such people can the Word be properly preached and the sacraments properly administered.

It is to a consideration of Bullinger's views on baptism and the Lord's Supper that we now turn. These are the only true sacraments Bullinger recognizes.

BAPTISM

Heinrich Bullinger preached on the subject of baptism in the fifth *Decade*, the eighth sermon. The title of that sermon gives its outline:

> Of Holy Baptism; What It Is; By Whom, And
> When It Was Instituted, And That There Is But
> One Baptism Of Water. Of The Baptism Of Fire.
> Of The Rite Or Ceremony Of Baptism; How, Of
> Whom, And To Whom It Must Be Ministered.
> Of Baptism By Midwives; And Of Infants Dying
> Without Baptism. Of The Baptism Of Infants.
> Against Anabaptism Or Re-Baptizing; And Of
> The Power Or Efficacy Of Baptism.[8]

That "wordy" title matches the wordiness and verbosity of the sermon itself. Bullinger had treated the subject of baptism, naturally, in a number of places in his occasional works and theological tractates. But here he considers it most fully in one place.

Like the vast majority of Christians of his time, Bullinger accepted the utility and correctness of infant baptism

---

7. Bullinger, *Decades*, 5:131.
8. Bullinger, *Decades*, 5:351.

and here gives its various justifications. In essence, baptism is to the church what circumcision was to Israel: the sign of inclusion in the people of God. As Bullinger puts it at the beginning of his sermon:

> They define baptism, for the most part, to be a token or recognizance of our cleansing, yea, of our enrolling, whereby we are received into the church to be of the number of God's children. But we, describing the nature of baptism more at large, do say; that it is an holy action instituted of God, and consisting of the word of God and the holy rite or ceremony whereby the people of God are dipped in the water in the name of the Lord: to be short, whereby the Lord himself doth represent and seal unto us our purifying or cleansing, gathereth us into one body, and putteth the baptized in mind of their duty.[9]

Bullinger, as can be seen, goes a bit further and suggests that baptism is not only the essential equivalent of circumcision but is also a call to the Christian to his or her duty. This is a regular feature of Bullinger's theology. He takes what's received, and he extends it further into Christian practice. It is one of the most remarkable aspects of his theology.

Time and space make it impossible to look more fully into each aspect of Bullinger's theology of baptism, but it is worth taking a few moments to investigate his denunciation of the re-baptizers, the Anabaptists.

He scathingly addresses the Anabaptists, after rejecting their suggestion that children were "logs" when baptized; passive and uninvolved:

> Go, ye false knaves, go with your blasphemies to the place which you deserve! It is a most filthy

9. Bullinger, *Decades*, 5:352.

> deed, yea, and more than barbarous, in that ye compare infants to logs; for what great store God setteth by infants, we taught you already before out of the gospel. But men, which now begin to have the use of sound reason, are diligently and earnestly to be taught and admonished to remember they are baptized, and to endeavour, by calling on the name of the Lord, in all points to be answerable in life and conversation to their promise and profession.[10]

He then remarks:

> But letting pass these brainsick, frantic, and foul-mouthed railers, who (as we have heard) never want words to wrangle, though we have had never so much, never so often, and never so earnest conference with them; let us proceed to declare in a few but yet manifest arguments, that infants are to be baptized, and that the apostles of Christ our Lord have baptized infants.[11]

And so he continues to explain why and how the baptism of infants is proper, biblical, apostolic, and rational. The Anabaptists, for their part, weren't having any of it and as time passed, positions hardened.

Bullinger, in sum, held to the same view of baptism as Luther, Zwingli, Calvin, Bucer, Oecolampadius, and the rest of the Lutheran and Reformed theologians of the sixteenth century. Is that true of his view of the Lord's Supper as well? Certainly not, for of the Lord's Supper he and Zwingli and Oecolampadius went their own way, against the Catholics and against the Lutherans. We turn then, next, to Bullinger's view of the Supper.

---

10. Bullinger, *Decades*, 5:388.
11. Bullinger, *Decades*, 5:388.

THE LORD'S SUPPER

The greatest rift between the budding Protestant and Reformed movements in Germany and Switzerland was caused by their different views of the meaning of the Lord's Supper. In an attempt to mollify all camps and find agreement (for purely political reasons) the Margrave, Philip, called a conference at Marburg to settle things between the leaders of the various camps. So Luther and Melanchthon on the Lutheran side and Zwingli and Oecolampadius, on the Swiss side, met and discussed things for three days in 1529, during the earliest days of October.

The conference, however, was a massive failure. Luther refused to so much as shake Zwingli's hand and even went so far as to insist that Zwingli wasn't a Christian. And Zwingli, for his part, left the conference with tears in his eyes.

Both men went home and published eviscerating denunciations of their conversation-partner's views. Luther continued to insist that the very body and blood were present in the Supper and Zwingli continued to insist that the bread and wine represented, symbolically, the body and blood of Christ. Though the fourteen Marburg articles agreed on thirteen points, the fourteenth was insurmountable and agreement could not be reached.

When Bullinger began writing on the subject of the Supper he adopted the Zwinglian viewpoint. And when he arrived in Zurich he continued to hold that position. And he did so even years later when he and Calvin hammered out the *Zurich Consensus*, to which we shall return.

Bullinger summarized his viewpoint on the Supper, briefly, which is an astonishing accomplishment for such a verbose theologian, in the Second Helvetic Confession. You can read the entire Confession online. In chapter 21 where he discusses the Supper, he writes of the elements themselves:

> We do not, therefore, so join the body of the Lord and his blood with the bread and wine as to say that the bread itself is the body of Christ except in a sacramental way; or that the body of Christ is hidden corporeally under the bread, so that it ought to be worshipped under the form of bread; or yet that whoever receives the sign, receives also the thing itself. The body of Christ is in heaven at the right hand of the Father; and therefore our hearts are to be lifted up on high, and not to be fixed on the bread, neither is the Lord to be worshipped in the bread. Yet the Lord is not absent from his Church when she celebrates the Supper. The sun, which is absent from us in the heavens, is notwithstanding effectually present among us. How much more is the Sun of Righteousness, Christ, although in his body he is absent from us in heaven, present with us, nor corporeally, but spiritually, by his vivifying operation, and as he himself explained at his Last Supper that he would be present with us (John, chs. 14; 15; and 16). Whence it follows that we do not have the Supper without Christ, and yet at the same time have an unbloody and mystical Supper, as it was universally called by antiquity.[12]

Bullinger's early statements on the Supper and his theology of the Supper are most thoroughly and clearly summarized, as has been the case throughout, in his sermon on the subject. The title of that sermon is:

---

12. https://www.creeds.net/reformed/helvetic/index.htm, accessed 16 November, 2020.

Of The Lord's Holy Supper; What It Is, By Whom, When, And For Whom It Was Instituted; After What Sort, When, And How Oft It Is To Be Celebrated, And Of The Ends Thereof. Of The True Meaning Of The Words Of The Supper, "This Is My Body." Of The Presence Of Christ In The Supper. Of The True Eating Of Christ's Body. Of The Worthy And Unworthy Eaters Thereof: And How Every Man Ought To Prepare Himself Unto The Lord's Supper.[13]

Bullinger addresses, in this unsurprisingly lengthy sermon, is the meaning of the Supper, its institution, its celebration, its meaning, the presence of Christ in it, what exactly is eaten when it is eaten, those who take part in an unworthy manner, and on examining oneself before taking part in it.

There is general agreement among all Christians that the celebration of the Lord's Supper is a commemoration of the sacrifice of Jesus. What Christians are literally putting in their mouths when they participate in the Supper is the point of contention. Is it literally blood and flesh? Or do the elements represent blood and flesh? For Lutherans and Catholics, it is the actual blood and flesh of Jesus, transformed into those very elements in the words of institution.

Bullinger thought not.

> The Lord, sitting at the self-same table with his disciples, reached the bread unto them with his own hand. And he, having only one true, human, and natural body, with the very same body of his delivered bread unto his disciples, and not a body either of any other man's, or that of his own.[14]

---

13. Bullinger, *Decades*, 5:401.
14. Bullinger, *Decades*, 5:438.

The body distributed was not Christ's body. It *represented* Christ's body. The very institution of the Lord's Supper itself teaches that the elements symbolize the presence of Christ. More fully, Bullinger insists:

> Wherefore those solemn words, "This is my body, which is broken for you;" and likewise, "This is my blood, which is shed for you;" can have none other sense than this: This is a commemoration, memorial, or remembrance, sign or sacrament, of my body which is given for you; This cup, or rather the wine in the cup, signifieth or represented unto you my blood which was once shed for you. For there followeth in the Lord's solemn words that which notably confirmeth this meaning: "Do this in the remembrance of me." As if he should say: Now am I present with you, before your eyes; I shall die and ascend up into heaven, and then shall this holy bread and wine be a memorial or token of my body and blood given and shed for you. Then break the bread and eat it, distribute the cup and drink it; and do this in the remembrance of me, praising my benefits bestowed on you in redeeming you and giving you life.[15]

The viewpoint of Bullinger and Zwingli is in point of fact the point of view of many Baptists today all around the world, and, so is a view held by vast numbers of Christians.

The Supper of the Lord and its meaning continued, however, to be a point of contention even among Reformed Christians, who struggled to understand this extremely important doctrine and who continued to refine their comprehension of it. Calvin and Bullinger discussed the topic at great length and over a period of months arrived at an agreement that, interestingly, carried forward the

---

15. Bullinger, *Decades*, 5:439.

viewpoint of Bullinger rather than Calvin, predominantly. That agreement, meant to unite the Reformed churches of the Swiss Confederation and Geneva, was called the "Zurich Consensus." We now turn to it, as it was, after the Second Helvetic Confession, Bullinger's greatest achievement.

THE ZURICH CONSENSUS[16]

As the Reformed continued to struggle to come to terms with the meaning of the Lord's Supper in contrast with the views of the Lutherans and the Catholics, Both Calvin and Bullinger put their hands to the task.

The first draft of what came to be known as the *Consensus Tigurinus* (The Zurich Consensus) was written by Calvin in 1548 with notes appended by Bullinger. This draft was rejected by the Swiss cantons, who felt that it still clung to the views of the Catholics too closely and so they requested Bullinger to rework it completely, which he did.

A draft was finally ready for discussion in 1549, and Calvin travelled to Zurich, along with Farel, to meet with Bullinger and hammer out the final details of the document. The Consensus was published in 1551 in Latin and translated and published by Bullinger into German and by Calvin into French.

The Consensus shows us a number of important things about Bullinger's great importance in the Reformed churches. It was not Calvin's draft that was accepted, it was Bullinger's. It was not Bullinger who travelled to Geneva to hammer out the final details but Calvin who travelled to Zurich. Calvin was clearly the junior partner in the enterprise.

---

16. https://www.creeds.net/reformed/Tigurinus/tigur-bunt.htm, accessed Nov 16, 2020.

HEINRICH BULLINGER

The Swiss loved the Consensus. But they were not the only ones:

> The Consensus was adopted by the Churches of Zurich, Geneva, St. Gall, Schaffhausen, the Grisons, Neuchatel, and, after some hesitation, by Basle, and was favorably received in France, England, and parts of Germany. Melanchthon declared to Lavater (Bullinger's son-in-law) that he then for the first time understood the Swiss, and would never again write against them; but he erased those passages of the Consensus which made the efficacy of the sacrament depend on election.[17]

Consequently, this episode in the history of the Reformed Church shows the immense power of Bullinger among Reformed Christians of the sixteenth century. A power and importance that have disappeared or been forgotten over time. For now, it is not Bullinger who is widely admired and appealed to, but Calvin.

Key articles of the Consensus are:

> Article Six: This spiritual communion which we have with the Son of God, when he lives in us by his Spirit, makes every believer a partaker of all the blessings which reside in him. To testify to this, the preaching of the gospel was instituted and the use of the sacraments was entrusted to us, namely the sacraments of holy Baptism and the holy Supper.

> Article Twenty-One: It is particularly necessary to reject every idea of a local presence. For as the signs are present in this world and are perceived with the eyes and touched with the hands, so

---

17. Schaff, *Creeds* 1: 473.

> Christ, as man, is nowhere but in heaven and is to be sought in no other way than by the mind and the understanding of faith. For this reason it is a perverse and impious superstition to enclose him under elements of this world.
>
> Article Twenty-Four: In this way not only the fiction of the Papists about transubstantiation is refuted, but also all stupid fantasies and worthless quibbles which either derogate from his heavenly glory or do not really agree with the truth of his human nature. And we judge that it is no less absurd to place Christ under the bread or to couple him with the bread than to transubstantiate the bread into his body.

The Consensus ties Bullinger's views of the sacraments together and makes his views accessible in the clearest, and briefest, possible form. The sermons he preached treat the topic more fully, but those looking for a clear and concise explanation can do no better than the Zurich Consensus.

QUESTIONS FOR DISCUSSION

1. In Bullinger's works, what is "The Word"?
2. How does Bullinger's understanding of baptism align with Reformed theology on the whole?
3. What do you think are the strengths and weaknesses of Zwingli and Bullinger's view of the Supper?

10

THE STATE AND LAST THINGS

It may seem, at first blush, that combining Bullinger's understanding of the state and eschatology (the doctrine of the "last things") in one chapter is a bit odd. But, hopefully in due course, it will become obvious why these two aspects of his thinking have been combined here. In short, for Bullinger, the state is the interim measure between the time of Christ and the return of Christ. The two, then, belong hand in glove.

Government in the Swiss cantons in the sixteenth century was not similar to American government in the twenty-first century. First of all, the Swiss cantonal system actually functioned quite efficiently. And second, in Zurich, two groups of magistrates guided the politics of the city and its surrounding canton. The larger group was responsible for matters concerning the populace at large, while the smaller group was responsible for weightier matters.

Representation in the councils was made up primarily of members of the various guilds and wealthy families who had, they believed, the largest stake in political matters. But the church was also represented and the notion of a separate church and state would never have occurred to anyone sensible. The church and the state were intermingled, or entangled, to such an extent that they were literally barely noticeable as separate entities.

After the horror of the Second Kappel War and the death of Zwingli, whom many held personally responsible for the fiasco because of his "war for freedom of religion" speeches, the Zurich magistrates (the governing officials) were extremely hesitant to take the advice of their religious leaders concerning matters of war and peace, and they curtailed their habit of listening to the pastor of the Great Minster and the other ministers of the large churches of Zurich, St. Peter's and the Fraumunster. Hence, when Bullinger arrived to take up the pastoral mantle left deserted by the dead Zwingli, he understood quite well that his political influence would be great, but not endless. And he acted accordingly.

Bullinger, that being said, was not afraid to bring matters to the attention of the magistrates and to demand that they do what Christian principles (of the Reformed variety) dictated. Bullinger was more than willing to confront the magistrates about such sundry matters as legislating church attendance, revising the poor laws, the marriage laws, and the divorce laws, and other things that touched Christian practice. But he shied away from giving advice about intercantonal policy and seems never to have advised military action in any respect.

Bullinger, like the rest of the "magisterial reformers" (who were called that not because they were majestic, but because their Reformation efforts were carried out with the full cooperation of their city's magistrates), needed the politicians to be on their side in order to get the proper laws passed, which would ensure that the people of their areas acted like Christians were supposed to act. Luther was successful because the princes of Germany, and in particular his own prince, were happy to throw egg in the face of the pope and the emperor. Calvin was successful in Geneva (once he returned for his second sojourn there) because the Genevan magistrates gave him free reign over the morals of the city. Zwingli had earlier been successful in Zurich because the magistrates—angry over a large payment that was promised from Rome but that never materialized—had a bone to pick with the pope.

Bullinger, similarly, was successful in large part because the canton's magistrates supported him (as he, it has to be said, also supported them from the pulpit). This, to us, rather odd intermixture of church and state was absolutely indispensable for the success of the Reformation and indicates why the magistrate features so widely throughout Bullinger's sermons. That is, according to the English edition of the *Decades*, Bullinger mentions the magistrates 187 times. By contrast, he mentions St. Jerome a scant thirteen times. The magistrates mattered. They were the state. What, then, does Bullinger have to say about them? That is the question to which we now turn.

THE MAGISTRATE IN BULLINGER'S THEOLOGY

Bullinger has, as described above, a lot to say about magistrates. In fact, he takes several sermons to address the topic, not to mention the many other references to magistrates throughout his works. So, for instance, in the Second Decade, the seventh sermon, he preaches:

> THE first and greatest thing, that chiefly ought to be in a magistrate, is easily perceived by the declaration of his office and duty. In my yesterday's sermon I shewed you what the magistrate

> is, how many kinds of magistrates there are, of whom the magistrate had his beginning, for what causes he was ordained, the manner and order how to choose peers, and what kind of men should be called to be magistrates. To this let us now add what the office and duty of a magistrate properly is.[1]

It is simply fascinating that Bullinger, realizing that the magistrates are indispensable for the spread of the gospel, insists that they meet certain requirements that have more to do with their spirituality than their governmental competence. It's better to have godly magistrates than it is to have politically minded and astute politicos. Bullinger expands on his description as follows:

> The whole office of a magistrate seemeth to consist in these three points; to order, to judge, and to punish: of every one whereof I mean to speak severally in order as they lie. The ordinance of the magistrate is a decree made by him for maintaining of religion, honesty, justice, and public peace: and it consisteth on two points; in ordering rightly matters of religion, and making good laws for the preservation of honesty, justice, and common peace. But before I come to the determining and ordering of religion, I will briefly, and in few words, handle their question which demand, whether the care of religion do appertain to the magistrate as part of his office or no? For I see many that are of opinion, that the care and ordering of religion doth belong to bishops alone, and that lungs, princes, and senators ought not to meddle therewith.[2]

1. Bullinger, *Decades*, 2:323.
2. Bullinger, *Decades*, 2:323.

Bullinger has in mind, and he makes this clear in the following sermon, that the magistrates are to order proper behavior, judge those who behave improperly, and punish those who need to be punished. In short, it is no exaggeration to suggest that the magistrate, in Bullinger's view, only exists to enforce church discipline. The church teaches morality and ethics and Christians are expected to live by those standards. If they do not, then the state exists to bring them back into line.

So, for instance, if a person fails to attend worship, and the Bible admonishes attendance, then the job of the magistrate is to order the non-attender to make himself or herself present at worship. If not, then punishment will follow. Whether that be a fine, or jail, or expulsion from the canton depends on how many services the sinner has skipped.

The state enforced the wishes of the church. Or that, at least, was how things were supposed to be, according to Bullinger and, it must be said, according to Calvin too. Broadly speaking, then, the magistrate was a servant of the church just as the ministers and clerics were; but with the power of the sword, not the pulpit. Both worked for God.

Bullinger also believed, and taught, that the magistrates alone were those responsible for protecting the flock of God, by means of war, if necessary. He remarked:

> To the right of the sword, which God hath given to the magistrate, doth war belong: for in my last sermon I taught you, that the use of the sword in the magistrate's hand is twofold, or of two sorts. For either he punisheth offenders therewith; or else repelleth the enemy that spoileth or would spoil his people, or cutteth off the rebellious purposes of his own seditious citizens.[3]

---

3. Bullinger, *Decades*, 2:370.

Ministers are not those tasked with war. This is the lesson Bullinger learned from the Second War of Kappel. There, Zwingli had made the tremendous error of taking upon himself the responsibility of calling for war and that error had fatal consequences, not only for Zwingli, but for the canton and the Reformed of the Swiss Confederation.

But Bullinger wasn't simply interested in discussing the place of the magistrate in the plan of God or whether or not the magistrate had the right to lead the people into war. He also was concerned with whether or not Christians should be magistrates and whether as Christian magistrates they had the duty to put people to death. In other words, should Christians be involved in the government, and if they are, should they take part in executions?

These questions arose because the Anabaptists were afoot, teaching that Christians should have no involvement in this world's doings and certainly they should not take part in any sort of killing, either in war as soldiers or in courts of law as executioners or judges. Bullinger was compelled to respond to these issues because of his firm belief that 1) the government needed Christian input and 2) Christians needed to be responsible members of the state, both as citizens and as those who hold public office in the government.

So, in accordance with his views, Bullinger preached, in the Second Decade, the eighth sermon titled:

> Of Judgment, And The Office Of The Judge; That Christians Are Not Forbidden To Judge: Of Revengement And Punishment: Whether It Be Lawful For A Magistrate To Kill The Guilty: Wherefore, When, How, And What The Magistrate Must Punish: Whether He May Punish Offenders In Religion Or No.[4]

---

4. Bullinger, *Decades*, 2:345.

that not only *could* Christians take part in government, they *must*. And if they occupy the magistracy or the office of the judge, they must carry those responsibilities fully.

He begins this sermon with these words:

> I SPAKE yesterday, dearly beloved, of the magistrate's ordinance: there are yet behind other two parts of his office and duty, that is, judgment and punishment; of both which, by the help of God, I mean to speak as briefly as may be. Give ye attentive ear, and pray ye to the Lord to give me grace to speak the truth.[5]

The heart of the matter is that God has instituted law and its enforcement because people are evil and need to be controlled, since they are incapable of controlling themselves.

> The Lord, I grant, commanded that which our adversaries have alleged; meaning thereby to settle quietness among his people: but because the malice of men is invincible, and the long-suffering of seemly souls makes wicked knaves more mischievous, therefore the Lord hath not forbidden nor condemned the moderate use of judgments in law.[6]

If people acted properly, law wouldn't be necessary. And Christians wouldn't need to be participants in government if government weren't needed. Sadly, however, because of human depravity, it is.

Bullinger's view of the magistrate and government writ large is that it is an interim measure, necessary to maintain decency while we await the return of Christ and

---

5. Bullinger, *Decades*, 2:345. This "brief" sermon runs from page 345 to 369, so it is not so brief after all.

6. Bullinger, *Decades*, 2:351.

the establishment of God's everlasting kingdom. It is to that topic that we now turn our attention.

THE LAST THINGS[7]

It is remarkable how little interest Bullinger shows for eschatology in the *Decades*. His only discussion is found in the Fourth *Decade*, the final (tenth) sermon, which he titles "Of The Reasonable Soul Of Man; And Of His Most Certain Salvation After The Death Of His Body."

This sermon extends from page 365 to page 408. His concluding paragraph is worth mentioning as it summarizes the tone and thrust of the entire sermon. He writes:

> To the omnipotent God therefore, our most merciful Father, and continual running fountain of all good graces and which is never drawn dry, who fashioned our body in our mother's womb, and breathed or poured into it a reasonable soul, which might whilst it is joined to the body quicken and direct us, and when it is separated from the body might forthwith after the death of the body be translated into heaven, there to live in joy and happiness until it return again unto the body being raised from the dead in the last judgment, with the which it may rejoice and be glad for ever and without end; to that God, I say, through Jesus Christ, for whose sake we are made partakers of so great a benefit, be glory, praise, and thanksgiving for evermore. Amen.[8]

Bullinger's eschatology, then centers itself on the reality of the continuing existence of the individual into

---

7. The "last things" are fully examined in Stephens, *Theology*, 449–82.

8. Bullinger, *Decades*, 4:408.

eternity, beyond death. In eternity, the individual's life is one of joy and happiness. And that joy and happiness extends through eternity where rejoicing and gladness are the chief characteristics of those so blessed.

To be sure, hell is real for Bullinger. But he spends far more time focusing on the destiny of the saints rather than the misery of the sinners. In his other works, Bullinger is far more expansive of his treatment of the topic of glory than of damnation.

The most extensive treatment of eschatology in the works of Bullinger is found in *The Christian Religion*. There he describes the death of the soul and the death of the body in some detail, mainly as he draws examples from Scripture. The death of the body happens to all whilst the death of the soul, the everlasting death of the soul, happens to those outside of grace. Bullinger is not a proponent of annihilationism nor is he a proponent of universalism. There are lost and there are redeemed. The lost are punished for their sins by dying forever in hell. The saved are those who are redeemed and though they die physically, they do not die everlastingly.

Bullinger also addresses the issue of illness and its hinting at and pointing towards death. Here, Bullinger is at his most pastoral. Stephens' summarizes this segment of the book so beautifully that it is worth repeating here:

> Bullinger holds before the sick examples from the New Testament but also Christ who is both example and saviour. Following James 5, the sick when gravely ill may send for the minister to instruct, strengthen, and console them. But ministers do not now anoint with oil, as anointing was linked with miraculous healing, and such miracles ceased after the time of the apostles. Bullinger's call is to forgive and not to show ill will or hatred. As we consider the way Christ

> responded to the way he was treated when arrested, tried, and crucified, we should strive to follow his example and pray for strength to follow his example of prayer, patience, not complaining, but offering his life for our salvation.[9]

Illness, in Bullinger's view, points not only towards death; but towards salvation. This perspective is immensely important as it marks a turning point in the theological understanding of both death and suffering.

But Bullinger also concerned himself with other issues related to eschatology besides death and redemption and the life everlasting. He also addressed one of the most pressing and important issues of his day: the subject of the "sleep of the soul."

Soul sleep, as a doctrinal concept, was fairly old by the time Bullinger came on the scene. It is the notion that when a person dies, they "go to sleep" until they are raised on the last day. It takes quite literally the New Testament phrase "asleep in the Lord." Beginning with Matthew 27:52's mention of those saints who had "fallen asleep" being raised on the day Jesus was and through Acts 7:60, which mentions Stephen's "death" as his "falling asleep," to Acts 13:36, where David is described as "falling asleep" and being buried, as well as 1 Corinthians 15:6, 18, 20, 1 Thessalonians 4:13, 15, and 2 Peter 3:4, texts were taken to mean literally being asleep.

Bullinger believed those who advocated "soul sleep" were wrong in believing that at death, Christians simply "fall asleep" and do not wake up until the coming of Christ. In this, Bullinger agreed with John Calvin who had written a book, *Psychopannychia* (1542), against this view. The church had previously condemned the doctrine of soul sleep at the Fifth Lateran Council (1513).

9. Stephens, *Bullinger's Theology*, 451.

The Reformers interpreted Paul's words that "we would rather be away from the body and at home with the Lord" (2 Cor 5:8) to mean that when we die, we enter into the presence of God—with no notion of "soul sleep" in which there is a period of unconsciousness ("sleep") before consciousness of being in the presence of God occurs. The emphasis of Paul—and the Protestant Reformers—was on resurrection! Those who die are raised directly into the presence of God.

Bullinger turned his attention to soul sleep (we might even call it a myth to be debunked) as early as the 1520s and 1530s. Indeed, in one of his earliest preserved letters (from 1526), wherein he answers the question of Paul Beck about soul sleep, Bullinger's answer is simple and direct: the soul does not sleep after death but lives consciously with Christ, in heaven while the body awaits its resurrection on the last day.[10]

The most stringent proponents of "soul sleep" in Bullinger's own day, and the people with whom he debates the topic most often, were the Anabaptists. In 1531, shortly after taking up the charge of the Great Minster in Zurich, Bullinger wrote his little volume *Anabaptist Teaching*. At the end of Part IV of this engaging and thorough volume, Bullinger works through carefully and meticulously the teaching of these "heretics" and "false teachers." His opinion, in fact, was that the Anabaptist view was a contradiction of the gospel itself. Thus, Bullinger defends in no uncertain terms what he considers to be the teaching of Scripture, both in opposition to the traditional acceptance of "soul sleep" and the inaccurate, in his view, teaching of the Anabaptists on the subject.

As in so many matters, Bullinger was waging a two-front doctrinal war. On the right were the Roman Catholics

10. *Briefwechsel*, Bd 1: 258.

and what he considered to be their doctrinal missteps and on the left were the followers of Luther and the Anabaptists. And Bullinger never flagged or wavered.

Another key issue for Bullinger and his compatriots and foes was the identity of the Antichrist and his being a harbinger of the end of time. For Bullinger and his Protestant contemporaries the Antichrist was not a figure coming to signal the end of time, he was the pope. As Bullinger makes clear in the Fifth Decade:

> But the pope's champions dispute, that it is for the profit and salvation, yea, necessary for the church, to have some one bishop to have pre-eminence over the other, both in dignity and power. But let them dispute and set forth this their idol as they please: they which will simply confess the truth must needs freely acknowledge, that the pope is antichrist; for that which these men babble of the supremacy of the pope is flatly repugnant to the doctrine of the gospel and of the apostles.[11]

Bullinger, along with Zwingli and Calvin and Luther as well as the other so called "minor" reformers, saw the pope and the papacy itself as an instrument of evil, as against Christ, as Antichrist. In distinction from much modern discussions of the Antichrist (especially in premillennialist circles) where Antichrist is conflated with "the Beast" in the Book of Revelation, that conflation was not part and parcel of sixteenth-century Reformed theology's system of thought.

How and when the world would come to an end and the new heavens and new earth be established was scarcely something Bullinger thought very much about. He had more pressing matters to attend to and the mystery of the

11. Bullinger, *Decades*, 5:122.

end was something that he was more than willing to leave as a mystery. Besides, even the Book of Revelation was not written primarily to describe the "when" of the end, but instead to comfort those living in the present.

Bullinger differed from many of the other Reformers in that he valued the Book of Revelation and indeed preached a series of sermons from it. There his focus was not on the end, but on the present, as, again, he saw the Book of Revelation as a source of comfort and encouragement for people living in the here and now. W. P. Stephens writes:

> In the preface to his Sermons on the Apocalypse Bullinger makes clear his purpose in preaching on the Apocalypse. His concern is to console and encourage those who are suffering persecution. The sermons are dedicated "to all the exiles for the name of Christ" and "to the all faithful everywhere looking for the coming of Christ the Lord and judge." Bullinger expresses his concern in various ways: that people will doubt God's goodwill towards them and fall again into idolatry, that they will be discouraged by the evils that afflict them and think that God's promises about the final end of good and evil and the deliverance of the faithful by the last judgment are vain. Bullinger describes the way the followers of the pope seek to suppress the gospel and drive simple people to abandon it. He maintains that it was for such hard times as this that Christ revealed the apocalypse to John.[12]

Comfort and consolation. Those two words nicely summarize the entire life's work of Heinrich Bullinger.

---

12. Stephens, *Theology*, 474.

Readers of Bullinger today too will be well rewarded with both comfort and consolation.

QUESTIONS FOR DISCUSSION

1. What is Bullinger's understanding of the State, and how does it differ from, or how is it similar to, your own?

2. What do you think of Bullinger's view of the "last things," and how is it similar to, and different from, your own?

3. How does Bullinger help you to wrestle with questions about death and an afterlife?

11

THE ABIDING SIGNIFICANCE OF HEINRICH BULLINGER

REFLECTING ON THIS SURVEY of Heinrich Bullinger's theology in this "gateway to Bullinger," we ask: what is the abiding significance of Heinrich Bullinger for today?

Bullinger was a major sixteenth-century theologian. He was a leader of the Protestant Reformation and an esteemed theological voice, known and respected throughout Europe. He developed his theology through his voluminous writings. We have tried to introduce the main themes of Bullinger's thought as clearly as possible so his views can be understood and considered today as Christians reflect on their faith.

When we think of Bullinger's abiding significance for today, we ask what emphases did he make that are in need of accenting and recovering today—in our churches and in our Christian lives? Here are some that seem vital to us.

IMPORTANCE OF SCRIPTURE

Bullinger saw himself first and foremost as a preacher of God's Word. His preaching ministry in Zurich extended decades and Bullinger's primary occupation was the reading and studying of Scripture. These studies were conveyed in his preaching ministry so the people of Zurich might know and understand what Scripture as the Word of God meant for their lives of faith day by day.

This communication of the Christian gospel—as understood through Scripture study—was at the core, at the very heart, of Bullinger's work as a theologian and a pastor. Scripture was foundational for hearing and understanding what God has done, what God is doing, and what God wants the people of God to do as disciples of Jesus Christ. Bullinger believed the Scriptures to be the means by which faith in Christ can be awakened, through the work of the Holy Spirit. The biblical message can transform human lives. So it is the most important thing in the world to communicate the message of Scripture to the world and make its message as clear as possible to Christian believers in the church. Through preaching and teaching, Bullinger stressed the importance of Scripture as the foundation that leads and guides the people of God into following God's ways and will. This was the work to which Heinrich Bullinger devoted his life. It can be rightly said that "through his preaching and writing, Bullinger sought to convey the message of the Bible. The whole enterprise of the Zurich reformation was based around the interpretation of scripture."[1]

The Bible is central to the church and for Christians today. We say with the Psalmist: "Your word is a lamp to my feet and a light to my path" (Ps 119:105). There are many resources to help Christians today to understand the Bible.

---

1. Gordon and Campi, *Architect*, 26.

Bullinger read the writings of theologians from the early church and the medieval period and used the tools of scholarship available to him. Our resources can include these and many more—to help us understand what the Scriptures meant and what they can mean for us in our contemporary contexts; and for our lives of faith. Bullinger's writings are filled with biblical references. He believed God's Word can communicate the reality of God—and the reality of Jesus Christ—by the power of the Holy Spirit and we can learn "how to live well and holily."[2]

IMPORTANCE OF CHRIST

The Scriptures point to Jesus Christ as God's Son who brings salvation to the world. For Bullinger, the Old Testament anticipated the coming of God's Messiah. The New Testament proclaims God's Messiah has come: Jesus Christ. Christ is the center of Scripture, for Bullinger.

The person of Jesus Christ leads to the work of Christ: the Son of God who was "crucified, dead, and buried" and "on the third day, he rose again from the dead"—as the Apostles' Creed puts it. This is the "good news," the message of the Christian gospel. Jesus Christ is, said Bullinger, "the sole Redeemer and Savior of the world, the King and High Priest, the true and awaited Messiah."[3] The Messiah is the redeemer and savior. He is king and high priest. As king, Christ is the ruler of all. As priest, Christ is the mediator between God and humanity and offers himself as the sacrifice for human sin. Salvation comes through faith in Christ—and this is the astonishing news of the Christian gospel! Jesus Christ—fully God and fully human—brings salvation—the restoration of the relationship between God

2. Bullinger, *Decades*, 1:56.
3. Cochrane, ed., *Reformed Confessions*, 246–47.

and humanity, which has been ruptured by human sin. This is the most important message in the world!

Bullinger stressed the centrality of Jesus Christ for theology and for Christian living. Followers of Jesus Christ receive the benefits of what Christ has done—in forgiveness of sin and reconciliation with God. They also live in service to Jesus Christ, being united with Christ by faith through the power of the Holy Spirit.

The church's message of incarnation: God becoming a human person in Jesus Christ; and salvation: Jesus' death for sinners to bring reconciliation with God—is the core of what the Scriptures teach and what the church proclaims. This is where Bullinger's focus was throughout his ministry; and where the church's focus should always be: on Jesus Christ—"Here is the Lamb of God who takes away the sin of the world!" (John 1:29).

IMPORTANCE OF THE FELLOWSHIP OF THE SAINTS

Bullinger's theology of predestination focused on Jesus Christ, whom Bullinger said was "predestinated or foreordained from eternity by the Father to be the Savior of the world."[4] Those who have "communion and fellowship with Christ" are saved, are elect.[5] The elect are the "church," the saints who live in a relationship of faith and union with Christ.

Christ came and died to "make one church and fellowship."[6] For the church is "the company, communion, congregation, multitude, or fellowship of all that profess the

---

4. Cochrane, ed., *Reformed Confessions*, 242.

5. Bullinger, *Decades*, 4:186. "If thou hast communion or fellowship with Christ, thou art predestinate to life, and thou art of the number of the elect and chosen," 187.

6. Bullinger, *Decades*, 3:259.

name of Christ."[7] The church as the whole company and multitude of the faithful" is "joined and united together as it were in one house and fellowship."[8] So the church is this fellowship of the saints who are united with Christ and with each other, in Christ.

In the church, the Word is preached and the sacraments are administered so the community hears God's Word and in the sacraments are reminded of what God has said and done. Bullinger's views of Word and sacraments has been formative in the United States and throughout the world.

Bullinger's theology of the church, seeing it as a "fellowship," is a vital reminder that those called by God are called into the "body of Christ" (1 Cor 12:27; Eph 4:12). The church is a corporate expression of the people of God who are committed to serving God in this world in Jesus Christ by the power of the Holy Spirit. Believers are called into a communal body to be united with Jesus Christ and with each other in a fellowship of faith.

Another way to put this is that for Bullinger there would be no "lone ranger Christianity"—a collection of individuals each doing one's "own thing" and all going their own ways based on their individual desires. Instead, as members of the "body of Christ," we "have fellowship with one another" (1 John 1:7). We share life with sisters and brothers in faith. Together, we listen to God's Word, seek God's will, and follow God's Spirit wherever we, in the church, are led to participate in witness and service. This conviction of the centrality of the church and the necessity of the church for Christian experience led Bullinger to declare in his Second Helvetic Confession:

---

7. Bullinger, *Decades*, 1:161.
8. Bullinger, *Decades*, 5:5.

> We esteem fellowship with the true Church of Christ so highly that we deny that those can live before God who do not stand in fellowship with the true Church of God, but separate themselves from it. For as there was no salvation outside Noah's ark when the world perished in the flood; so we believe that there is no certain salvation outside Christ, who offers himself to be enjoyed by the elect in the Church; and hence we teach that those who wish to live ought not to be separated from the true Church of Christ.[9]

In a culture where "individualism" is prized, faith in Jesus Christ draws us into the "community of saints"—called in the Apostles' Creed, "the communion of saints." This is the church, in which we share a common faith and common life together as disciples of Jesus Christ.

IMPORTANCE OF THE CHRISTIAN LIFE

The church is the body of believers in which our own Christian lives take shape. Our lives in Jesus Christ have an ecclesial context. We seek to be true to the call of God to all believers to serve God and hear Jesus Christ say, "Follow me" (Mark 2:14).

Bullinger and the other Protestant reformers were clear that while we are justified by faith alone—and receive the gift of salvation; we are not justified by a faith "which is alone." That is, our faith expresses itself in "good works"—in those ways of loving and serving others in which we seek to serve others as God in Jesus Christ served us. As Jesus said to his disciples: "I am among you as one who serves" (Luke 22:27). Disciples follow their Master. Those who love Jesus Christ will serve others, as Jesus served others.

---

9. Cochrane, ed., *Reformed Confessions*, 266.

For Bullinger, there is an inseparable unity between Christian belief and Christian action; between what we believe and what we do. Christian doctrine and Christian theology are not just matters of the "mind." They are also matters of the "heart." They are also matters of the "hands." Our belief expresses itself in actions—acts of love and service to others. As Paul put it: "The only thing that counts is faith working through love" (Gal 5:6).

Our "good works" are acts of love toward others. They express our faith and are pleasing to God, as well as ways of serving others. We are reminded of Paul's words: "For we are what he has made us, created in Christ Jesus for good works, which God prepared beforehand to be our way of life" (Eph 2:10). God calls people of faith to do good works to express the reality of their faith through their actions. As Bullinger put it, "For wheresoever faith is, there also it sheweth itself by good works" and "True faith is the wellspring and root of all virtues and good works."[10] For, "truly good works grow out of a living faith by the Holy Spirit and are done by the faithful according to the will or rule of God's Word."[11]

We are called to believe and to express our beliefs in good works—the chief of which is showing love. As Paul said, "love is the fulfilling of the law" (Rom 13:10). Bullinger said love springs from faith and love contains in itself "the sum of all good works." For "unless we have a true faith in God, there is no charity [love] in us."[12]

Bullinger's focus on our lives of service to God in Christ—doing "good works"—not as a *means to* salvation,

---

10. Bullinger, *Decades*, 1:118, 120.

11. Cochrane, ed., *Reformed Confessions*, 258. For Bullinger, those who have new life in Jesus Christ are liberated from sin and "free" to do good works.

12. Bullinger, *Decades*, 1:121.

but as an *expression of* salvation—is of the essence of Christian life. The church lives by its service to Jesus Christ. Its members live by their service to Jesus Christ by embodying love, which is "the sum of all good works," as Bullinger said.

ABIDING SIGNIFICANCE

Heinrich Bullinger provides a solid, robust theology, grounded in the Scriptures and historic traditions of the Christian church. He urges the focus of faith to be on God's love in sending Jesus Christ through whom we have forgiveness of sins and into whose service we can commit our lives. We are joined with other believers in the fellowship of the church which is nurtured and led by God's Word and Spirit. We are called to live out our faith in Christ by doing the works God calls us to do—most importantly in living lives of love which is God's will for us all!

QUESTIONS FOR DISCUSSION

1. What emphases of Bullinger's about Holy Scripture do you see as important for today?

2. What are key elements in Bullinger's understanding of the person and work of Jesus Christ that are significant for today?

3. What are ways that Bullinger's views of the church and Christian life can impact contemporary Christians?

4. Overall, what do you see as the "abiding significance" of Heinrich Bullinger for theology and for Christians today?

SELECTED BIBLIOGRAPHY

PRIMARY SOURCES

Bromiley, G. W., ed. *Zwingli and Bullinger*. Library of Christian Classics. Louisville, KY: Westminster John Knox , 2006.

Bullinger, Heinrich. Primary sources available at the Post-Reformation Digital Library. Online: http://www.prdl.org/author_view.php?a_id=175&source=primary. These sources include Bullinger's *Decades*, his sermons, the *Commonplaces*, tractates, and other important writings.

———. *Briefwechsel*. Online: http://teoirgsed.uzh.ch/.

Schaff, Philip *The Creeds of Christendom, with a History and Critical Notes*, 3 volumes. New York: Harper & Brothers, 1882.

SECONDARY SOURCES

Alfani, Guido, ed. *Famine in European History*. Università Commerciale Luigi Bocconi, Milan. Cambridge: Cambridge University Press, 2017.

Calvin, John. *Institutes of the Christian Religion*. Edited by John T. McNeill; translated by Ford Lewis Battles. Library of Christian Classics. Philadelphia: Westminster, 1960.

Cochrane, Arthur C., ed. *Reformed Confessions of the Sixteenth Century*. Historical introductions by Arthur Cochrane; new introduction by Jack Rogers. Louisville, KY: Westminster John Knox, 2003.

Dowey, Edward A. Jr., *A Commentary on the Confession of 1967 and an Introduction to "The Book of Confessions."* Philadelphia: Westminster, 1968.

Gordon, Bruce, and Emidio Campi, eds. *Architect of Reformation: An Introduction to Heinrich Bullinger 1504–1575*. Reprint, Eugene, OR: Wipf and Stock, 2019.

Harding, Thomas, ed. *The Decades of Henry Bullinger*, Volumes 1–2. Reprint, Charleston, SC: Nabu, 2010.

Holder, Ward R. *A Companion to Paul in the Reformation*. Brill's Companions to the Christian Tradition, 15. Boston: Brill, 2009.

McGrath, Alister. *Iustitia Dei: A History of the Christian Doctrine of Justification*. 4th ed. Cambridge: Cambridge University Press, 2020.

Muller, Richard A. *Christ and the Decree: Christology and Predestination in Reformed Theology from Calvin to Perkins*. Reprint, Grand Rapids: Baker, 1988.

Rogers, Jack B., and Donald K. McKim. *The Authority and Interpretation of the Bible: An Historical Approach*. Reprint, Eugene, OR: Wipf & Stock, 1999.

Stephens, William Peter. *The Theology of Heinrich Bullinger*. Edited by Jim West and Joe Mock. Reformed Historical Theology, 59. Göttingen: Vandenhoeck & Ruprecht, 2019.

Venema, Cornelis P. *Heinrich Bullinger and the Doctrine of Predestination*. Texts and Studies in Reformation and Post-Reformation Thought. Grand Rapids: Baker Academic, 2002.

Wallace, Dewey D. Jr., "Federal Theology." In *Encyclopedia of the Reformed Faith*, edited by Donald K. McKim and David F. Wright. Louisville, KY: Westminster/John Knox, 1992. Online: https://www.biblia.work/dictionaries/federaltheology/.

www.ingramcontent.com/pod-product-compliance
Lightning Source LLC
Chambersburg PA
CBHW020849160426
43192CB00007B/843